Linking Sustainable Community Activities to Pollution Prevention

A Sourcebook

Beth E. Lachman

Prepared for the Office of Science and Technology Policy

Critical Technologies Institute
RAND

This report provides a simple introduction to community sustainability activities and ways in which supporters of pollution prevention (P2) can take advantage of such efforts. It is based on a presentation entitled "The Sustainable Community Movement and P2," which the author presented at the National Pollution Prevention Roundtable (NPPR) Conference on April 11, 1996. This document should be of interest to state and local government P2 practitioners because of the synergy between community sustainability activities and their P2 efforts. Other organizations and individuals who are interested in sustainable communities and/or P2 should also find it helpful.

The report is based on the author's research, especially her work helping with the development and implementation of the National Environmental Technology Strategy (NETS). NETS is intended to promote the development and implementation of environmental technologies for a sustainable future. The author's research for the NETS was sponsored by the White House Office of Science and Technology Policy through RAND's Critical Technologies Institute (CTI).

CTI was created in 1991 by an act of Congress. It is a federally funded research and development center operated by RAND. CTI's mission is to

- Help improve public policy by conducting objective, independent research and analysis to support the Office of Science and

Technology Policy in the Executive Office of the President of the United States;

- Help decisionmakers understand the likely consequences of their decisions and choose among alternative policies; and

- Improve understanding in both the public and private sectors of the ways in which technological efforts can better serve national objectives.

CTI research focuses on problems of science and technology policy that involve or affect multiple Executive Branch agencies, different branches of the U.S. government, or interaction between the U.S. government and states, other nations, or the private sector.

This report is accessible on the World Wide Web at http://www.rand.org/publications/MR/MR855. Inquiries regarding CTI or this document may be directed to:

Bruce Don
Director, Critical Technologies Institute
RAND
1333 H St., N.W.
Washington, D.C. 20005
Phone: (202) 296-5000
Web: http://www.rand.org.cti
Email: cti@rand.org

CONTENTS

Preface iii

Summary vii

Acknowledgments xi

Acronyms xiii

Chapter One
INTRODUCTION 1
Background and Motivation 1
Objectives of This Report 3
How the Report Is Organized 3

Chapter Two
THE SUSTAINABLE COMMUNITY "MOVEMENT" 5
What Is Sustainability? 5
What Is a Sustainable Community? 6
What Is the Sustainable Community "Movement?" 8

Chapter Three
ELEMENTS OF SUSTAINABLE COMMUNITIES 13
Process of Developing a Sustainable Community 13
Developing an Ongoing Governance Structure 14
Creating a Vision 14
Setting Goals and Objectives 14
Developing Guiding Principles 15
Choosing and Implementing Activities 15
Evaluating Progress and Revising Activities 16

Organizing for Sustainability   16
   EcoVillage at Ithaca   17
   Cambridge Civic Forums   18

Chapter Four
RESOURCES FOR SUSTAINABILITY EFFORTS   21
Federal Government   21
State Governments   25
Local Governments   26
Industry and Professional Associations   28
Universities   28
Non-Governmental Organizations   29

Chapter Five
SUSTAINABLE COMMUNITY EXAMPLES   33
A Geographical Sample of Sustainable Community
     Projects   33
Four Community Examples   34
   Northampton County, Virginia   35
   Seattle, Washington   37
   EcoVillage at Ithaca, New York   40
   Presidio National Park   41

Chapter Six
RELATIONSHIPS BETWEEN SUSTAINABLE
COMMUNITY AND P2 ACTIVITIES   45
Definition of Pollution Prevention   45
How Sustainable Community Activities Incorporate P2 . .   47
Relevance of Sustainable Community Efforts for P2
     Activities   48
Taking Advantage of Sustainable Community Activities . .   49
Suggested Steps for Taking Action   52

Chapter Seven
CONCLUSION   55

ANNOTATED BIBLIOGRAPHY   59

Many communities across the United States are taking a new approach to developing long-term healthy communities based on the concepts of sustainability. Some have even called this process a sustainable community "movement." This report discusses the growing sustainable community "movement." Its purpose is to shed some light on this movement, to describe a range of efforts currently under way in U.S. communities, to explain the relationship of such efforts to pollution prevention (P2) activities, and to act as a reference source about sustainable communities for P2 practitioners and other individuals interested in these topics.

WHAT IS A "SUSTAINABLE COMMUNITY?"

The term "sustainable," particularly when paired with "community," has been used in a variety of contexts to denote a wide range of activities. The "sustainable community" concept has been applied to issues as varied as urban sprawl, new economic development, inner-city and brownfield redevelopment, local small businesses, a strong local economy, environmental justice, ecosystem management, recycling, agriculture, biodiversity, lifestyles, green buildings, energy conservation, and pollution prevention. This diversity in activities has helped cause confusion about the definition of the term. Simply defined, for this report, "sustainable community" refers to community efforts to address problems by:

- Taking a systems approach that attempts to deal holistically with economic, social, and environmental concerns;

- Adopting a long-term focus; and

- Building consensus and fostering partnership among key stake-holders about community problems and solutions.

There is a sustainable community "movement" in the sense that hundreds of communities across the United States have found that piecemeal approaches to community issues have not been adequate for solving their problems. This realization has led many communities to embrace some version of the "sustainable community" approach to deal with their most pressing problems. However, most experts agree that in the United States a community does not exist that has achieved sustainability, namely, a community with comprehensive environmental, social, and economic health and stability for many generations to come. Communities are trying to evolve toward sustainability and more sustainable practices.

DEVELOPING A SUSTAINABLE COMMUNITY

Communities take many different approaches in developing their sustainable community activities. However, the process usually includes the following types of steps:

- Develop a governance structure for the effort. This can be as simple as a steering committee or as complex as a series of committees and task forces.

- Create a shared vision of what a sustainable community will mean. This vision often attempts to imagine what participants want their community to look like in 20, 50, or 100 years.

- Set goals and objectives and formulate indicators of progress in achieving them. This step involves translating the vision into specific goals and milestones. It also tries to incorporate ongoing assessment measures into the project.

- Develop guiding principles. Once the goals are formulated, communities may devise a set of principles to guide them in the pursuit of their goals.

- Choose and implement activities. With goals and guiding principles to inform their efforts, communities determine what specific activities they will undertake and how they will go about them.

- Evaluate progress and revise activities accordingly. Finally, the process is generally viewed as evolutionary. As progress occurs (or does not occur), goals and objectives may need to be modified, or an implementation strategy changed.

An important part of this process is finding resources to support the community efforts. Resources for sustainability projects include information, funding, materials, expertise, and labor. Such resources can be obtained from many different sources including federal, state, and local governments; industry; universities; and non-governmental organizations (NGOs). Political support, community support, and management and government agency commitment to partner in the work are other important factors in this process.

SUSTAINABLE COMMUNITIES AND POLLUTION PREVENTION

Pollution prevention has been going on in this country for many years, frequently without any specific connection to sustainable community activities. Yet pollution prevention efforts have begun increasingly to merge with sustainable community efforts. This is true in large part because P2 has been a major building block for many communities' sustainability projects. P2 is frequently a goal or guiding principle for communities and may also provide a focus for specific activities. The vision of sustainable community projects can serve as an overarching vision for pollution prevention activities. These P2 activities are incorporated into the broader community perspective for developing a long-term healthy community. Sustainability projects also offer a way to harmonize industry, government, and general public efforts to address environmental issues, including P2 activities.

These sustainability efforts present important opportunities for pollution prevention practitioners, especially in state and local governments. It can enable them to educate a broader segment of the public about the benefits of P2 and thereby generate increased support for it. The link with sustainability can also help focus P2 efforts on difficult long-term or multidisciplinary problems, such as urban sprawl, and allow P2 to be integrated with other key community environmental management efforts. This link can facilitate innovative partnerships among different levels of government, the private sector, and other key players in addressing a wide range of community problems.

Many sources are available to P2 practitioners to learn more about sustainable community efforts. They range from traditional academic and technical literature to the hands-on practical experience of those who are implementing sustainability. The references for such information include academic, trade association, community and environmental groups, government literature, and World Wide Web (WWW) sites. The P2 practitioner can use such information to expand and enhance community P2 activities in coordination with sustainable community efforts.

Finally, the sustainable community movement is likely to continue and to grow. As it does, P2 efforts seem likely both to add impetus to the movement and to benefit from increased community interest in sustainability.

ACKNOWLEDGMENTS

The author would like to thank the many sustainable community and pollution prevention practitioners who provided information for this document, including representatives from federal, state, and local governments; non-government organizations; universities; and industry. This final report gained greatly from the thoughtful reviews by Margaret Reich of the Pollution Prevention Program, City of Portland, Oregon, and RAND colleague Joseph Bolten. The author would also like to thank Dave Adamson and Jerry Sollinger for their editorial and structural help with this document.

Any errors of fact and judgment are those of the author. Views and suggestions expressed here are not necessarily those of RAND or any of its sponsors.

AAES   American Association of Engineering Societies

AIA   American Institute of Architects

CBEP   Community-Based Environmental Protection

CERF   Civil Engineering Research Foundation

CTI   Critical Technologies Institute

DEP   Department of Environmental Protection (Florida)

DEQ   Department of Environmental Quality (Virginia)

DOC   Department of Commerce

DOE   Department of Energy

DOI   Department of the Interior

EDF   Environmental Defense Fund

EIP   Eco-Industrial Park

EPA   Environmental Protection Agency

FGDC   Federal Geographic Data Committee

IBACOS   Integrated Building and Construction Solutions

ICMA   International City/County Management Association

NACo   National Association of Counties

NETS   National Environmental Technology Strategy

NGO   Non-Governmental Organization

NIST   National Institute of Standards and Technology

NLC   National League of Cities

NOAA   National Oceanic and Atmospheric Administration

NPPR   National Pollution Prevention Roundtable

NPS   National Park Service

NSDI   National Spatial Data Infrastructure

NSTC   National Science and Technology Council

OEA   Office of Environmental Assistance (Minnesota)

OSEC   Office of Sustainable Ecosystems and Communities

P2   Pollution Prevention

PCSD   President's Council on Sustainable Development

POC   Points of Contact

PTI   Public Technology, Inc.

SAMP   Special Area Management Plan (Northampton County, Virgina)

STIP   Sustainable Technologies Industrial Park (Northampton County, Virginia)

USCM   United States Conference of Mayors

USDA   United States Department of Agriculture

USGS   United States Geological Survey

WWW   World Wide Web

Chapter One

INTRODUCTION

This report explores the relationship between sustainable community activities and pollution prevention (P2). It is oriented toward those in state and local government who deal with P2 because of the potential synergy that can occur between community sustainability activities and P2 efforts. Other organizations and individuals interested in either sustainable communities or P2 should also find it helpful. This document is based on a presentation given at the National Pollution Prevention Roundtable (NPPR)[1] Conference held in Washington, D.C., April 10–12, 1996.

BACKGROUND AND MOTIVATION

Two series of events crystallized some of the problems surrounding the sustainable community movement and provided the motivation for this report. The first series was the development and initial implementation of the National Environmental Technology Strategy. From summer 1994 through spring 1995 the National Science and Technology Council (NSTC)[2] sponsored a series of policy workshops, broader symposia, and a White House Conference on Environmental

---

[1]NPPR (the Roundtable) is the largest membership organization in the United States devoted solely to pollution prevention. It provides a national forum for promoting the development, implementation, and evaluation of efforts to avoid, eliminate, or reduce pollution at the source. The Roundtable's voting membership includes state, local, and tribal government pollution prevention programs. Affiliate members include representatives from federal agencies, nonprofit groups, and private industry.

[2]NSTC, a cabinet-level council, is the principal means for the President to coordinate science, space, and technology policies across the federal government.

Technology to gain stakeholder input into the development of the *Bridge to a Sustainable Future: National Environmental Technology Strategy*.[3] More than 10,000 participants from industry, environmental groups, academia, and state and local governments attended over 30 events held throughout the country. From participant input at these many events, the theme of sustainable communities emerged. Since then, more and more communities in the United States and throughout the world are conducting some sort of sustainability project.

Three points emerged from analyzing this development and implementation process and ongoing community efforts. First, in spite of the author's skepticism about the existence of a sustainable community movement, the response to the process of developing and implementing the national strategy and the range of community activities made it clear that such a movement exists, albeit in a diffuse and uncoordinated form. Second, it became clear that considerable confusion surrounds the definition of terms related to sustainability, particularly "sustainable community." Each community uses a slightly different definition and some use a different term altogether. However, their activities have many elements in common. The differences in terms are especially confusing to people who are just learning about such activities. Third, it became clear that many of the communities involved in sustainability activities are unaware of what other communities are doing along the same lines.

The second series of events was the NPPR conferences. The same confusion about the meaning of the term "sustainable community" was observed at these conferences. Furthermore, there was a lack of understanding about the relationship between sustainable community activities and pollution prevention activities. At the same time, many P2 practitioners and sustainable community practitioners were using P2 as a building block in their sustainable community activities. There appeared to be many potential benefits for P2 professionals from sustainable community activities and synergism between the two types of activities. There also was more and more

---

[3] *Bridge to a Sustainable Future: National Environmental Technology Strategy*, U.S. Government Printing Office, Washington, D.C., April 1995. To obtain a copy of this document, call 1-800-ENV-6676 or access on the World Wide Web (WWW) at: http://www.gnet.org/gnet/gov/usgov/whitehouse/bridge/bridge.htm.

interest in sustainability among P2 practitioners and others who view community relationships and challenges in a holistic manner. For these reasons, there seemed to be a need for a document providing sustainable community information for the P2 practitioner.[4]

OBJECTIVES OF THIS REPORT

This report defines the term "sustainable community" to help dispel some of the confusion about such community efforts. It describes a range of sustainable community activities to help provide communities with more information about what others are doing. It also identifies benefits for P2 practitioners and provides reference material about sustainable communities for supporters of P2, including information about resources, documents, and points of contact.[5]

HOW THE REPORT IS ORGANIZED

The next chapter presents working definitions for sustainability and the sustainable community and describes the "movement." To help set the context for how such initiatives are created and implemented, Chapter Three discusses basic elements in the sustainable community process, such as their development and organizational focuses. Then the report describes the sources of resources available for sustainable community projects in Chapter Four. Next, Chapter Five offers four examples of specific community sustainability efforts. Chapter Six provides a brief overview of the relationship between sustainable community activities and P2 activities. This chapter also provides suggestions for taking action, namely, how P2 promoters

---

[4]Throughout this report, the term "P2 practitioner" is used to refer to state and local government officials as well as other individuals supporting, promoting, and/or practicing pollution prevention. However, other individuals with interests in sustainability and P2 can also be considered P2 practitioners by this definition, since the term is meant to capture those who have any interest in integrating P2 practices and sustainable community efforts.

[5]The information provided here was accurate to the best of the author's knowledge when the document was published. However, some of the information, such as the WWW page addresses, may have changed since its publication. Please contact the author with any corrections or additions. The author welcomes any additional input about sustainable community activities and references.

can use sustainable community activities to enhance their own efforts. Chapter Seven provides a brief conclusion.

The report also contains an annotated bibliography that provides points of contact (POC), WWW page addresses, and documents about sustainable community activities. These references were chosen as a small sample of the many different resources available about sustainable communities.

Chapter Two

THE SUSTAINABLE COMMUNITY "MOVEMENT"

This chapter attempts to dispel some of the confusion surrounding the terminology used by those involved in the sustainable community movement. It provides working definitions for "sustainability" and "sustainable community" and it describes the sustainable community movement.

WHAT IS SUSTAINABILITY?

Disagreement exists about the precise meaning of the term "sustainability." The term is used in many contexts, including development, cities, agriculture, economy, technology, environment, buildings, etc. Confusion exists about the meaning of the term, since it is used in so many different contexts and often is defined differently. The most common starting definition is the one for sustainable development from the United Nations' World Commission on Environment and Development (the Bruntland Commission) 1987 report, *Our Common Future:*

> development that meets the need of the present without compromising the ability of future generations to meet their own needs.[1]

The term "sustainable development" may have a negative connotation because it is overused and is often associated with development in other countries, rather than in the United States. Also, some feel

---

[1] *Our Common Future,* World Commission on Environment and Development (the Bruntland Commission), Oxford University Press, Oxford, 1987, p. 43.

that using the word "development" overemphasizes economic issues. Furthermore, the term "sustainable development" does not necessarily recognize the importance of the local community. The term "sustainable community" is often defined slightly differently because it focuses on the sense of community and its importance. Cities and towns across the United States are often more comfortable with the term "sustainable cities" or "sustainable communities." Since rural areas, small towns, and suburban areas also implement sustainability projects, the term sustainable community applies more widely. For these reasons, the term sustainable community is used throughout this report. However, some people may use these terms interchangeably, and some of the sustainable community efforts presented here are known by one of these or some other alternative term.

WHAT IS A SUSTAINABLE COMMUNITY?

The term "sustainable community" is often defined uniquely by each community, on the basis of its individual interests, needs, and culture. Most sustainable community definitions focus on long-term integrated systems approaches, healthy communities, and quality-of-life issues by addressing economic, environmental, and social issues. The concept recognizes that economic, environmental, and social issues are interdependent and integrated. To stress the importance of addressing and balancing these issues, many have used the analogy of a three-legged stool. The legs of the stool represent economic, social, and environmental components and the seat is sustainability. If any of the three are not healthy, then the stool falls over and sustainability cannot ever be achieved.

Economic issues include good jobs, good wages, stable businesses, appropriate technology development and implementation, business development, etc. If a community does not have a strong economy, then it cannot be healthy and sustainable over the long term.

From an environmental standpoint, a community can be sustainable over the long term only if it is not degrading its environment or using up finite resources. Environmental concerns include protecting human and environmental health; having healthy ecosystems and habitat; reducing and/or eliminating pollution in water, air, and land; providing green spaces and parks for wildlife, recreation, and other uses; pursuing ecosystem management; protecting biodiversity; etc.

A community must also address social issues. If a community has significant social problems, such as serious crime, then it cannot be healthy and stable over the long term. Furthermore, such a community probably will not be able to address other key community issues, such as environmental problems, because it is so busy dealing with its social problems. Social issues addressed in sustainable community efforts include education, crime, equity, inner-city problems, community building, spirituality, environmental justice, etc. Since this report is focusing on P2 activities, the social issues are not emphasized. However, social issues are considered an important leg of the sustainability stool.

A major assumption of the sustainable community definition is that trying to address such issues in isolation eventually ends up hurting some other part of the community's health. For example, if a community focuses only on economic issues, the environment usually suffers. Only by addressing such issues in an integrated fashion can a healthy community be developed which can thrive for the next 10, 20, 50, and 100 years or more.

Most communities also recognize that sustainability is an evolutionary process. Currently, most experts agree that in the United States a sustainable community does not exist that has achieved sustainability, namely, a community with comprehensive environmental, social, and economic health and stability for many generations to come. Communities are evolving toward sustainability and more sustainable practices. Creating sustainability is a learning process.

Most sustainable community efforts also involve an open process in which every member of the community is encouraged to participate. The focus is on consensus building for the community. The emphasis is on communication and cooperation among many different interests and stakeholders from the community and also from those outside the geographic community if their actions might affect the community. Compromise by special interests is also key where necessary. All the different segments of the community at the local and regional level, including businesses, individuals, environmental and community groups, and government, need to work together cooperatively to move toward sustainability. There is also the recognition that communities are not isolated; they are interdependent with their region, the country, and the world. The phrase, "Think long term and globally, and act locally" applies.

This open participatory process focuses on communication, cooperation, and compromise by many different stakeholders to build consensus. Stakeholders include the general public, academia, industry, government, environmental groups, and community groups. Such a process frequently is very time consuming and may take years to develop. Often many public community meetings are held as part of this process as the different groups learn to trust, communicate with, and listen to one another.

Another critical dimension to creating a sustainable community is fostering a sense of community. Such sustainability activities try to enhance individuals' and organizations' feelings of attachment, value, and connection to the community. Many experts feel that only by caring about and feeling a part of their neighborhood, town, county, and/or city will individuals truly work together over the long term to develop a healthy community.

To summarize, a sustainable community effort consists of a long-term integrated and systems approach to developing and achieving a healthy community by addressing economic, environmental, and social issues. Fostering a strong sense of community is also an important part of such efforts. This definition is the one used throughout this report. Note that others may not define this term in quite the same way.

WHAT IS THE SUSTAINABLE COMMUNITY "MOVEMENT?"

Hundreds of communities throughout the United States and the world are developing sustainability projects and implementing more sustainable practices because of critical environmental and community problems facing them locally, regionally, nationally, and globally. They recognize that many of these problems, such as urban sprawl, cut across many different segments of the community and society. These problems cannot easily be solved by traditional approaches or traditional elements within our society. Many people feel it is better to address such problems through a new collaborative and holistic systems approach because such problems are multi-disciplinary, multi-agency, multi-stakeholder, and multi-sector in nature. The sustainable community approach—in a collaborative process focused on current and future generations' needs by integrating social, economic, and environmental issues—provides a promising opportunity to address such problems.

Since many sustainable community efforts have just begun, it is unclear whether this new approach will be successful. However, some efforts are making initial progress.[2] Evaluating the success of such efforts, however, is outside the scope of this report.

The focus and scale of sustainability efforts depend on many factors, including resources, how the effort was started, local politics, individual actions, and the unique needs and wants of the community. To illustrate this point, consider sustainability activities in Arlington, Virginia, and Chattanooga, Tennessee.

Arlington, Virginia, has had a grassroots neighborhood sustainability effort, called Arlington Community Sustainability Network, without any official government participation. Small groups of community members met monthly and developed and implemented projects that made their community more sustainable. Their activities primarily focused on the behavior of individuals in their homes and schools. For example, they focused on public schools as users and teachers of sustainable practices, such as installing solar hot water heaters at schools and a "Neighborhood Backyard Program" for children. They also sponsored an Arlington Energy Fair in 1993 and drafted the document "50 Things You Can Do to Build a Stronger Community."[3]

---

[2]Public Technology, Inc. (PTI) has created a Sustainable Communities Database, which includes descriptors of over 1,450 initiatives in 744 U.S. cities and counties. PTI has identified progress in some of these community efforts. Furthermore, for ten case studies of these sustainable communities projects, PTI briefly assesses their performance and transferability. Public Technology, Inc., *Cities and Counties: Thinking Globally, Acting Locally, Sustainability in Action*, 1996. For other examples of initial success see the bibliography at the end of this report.

[3]The Arlington Community Sustainability Network no longer officially exists. However, some of the ideas and activities started by this group have been incorporated into other community group activities.

The City of Chattanooga and Hamilton County, Tennessee, have a comprehensive sustainable community activity which involves many members of local government, businesses, and community groups. In response to the dual problems of inner-city decline and severe environmental degradation, the City of Chattanooga has incorporated sustainable community concepts into its development planning process. By focusing on the region's natural assets in its rivers, mountains, and waterfront area, all community members—citizens, business leaders, government, and community organizations—try to pay close attention to the interconnectedness of all aspects of community life. For example, Chattanooga is implementing projects to reduce air pollution and congestion and improve quality of life by reducing dependence on automobiles and by developing and implementing electric transit vehicles as part of an innovative transportation plan. Its activities also include preserving open space, watershed management, waste reuse and recycling, and cleaning up a polluted industrial site and creating a zero emissions manufacturing zone, also called an eco-industrial park,[4] at that site.

As these two examples illustrate, the types of issues addressed in sustainable community projects can vary significantly. Issues addressed by sustainability projects include urban sprawl, new economic development, inner-city and brownfield redevelopment, environmentally sound local small businesses, a strong local economy, eco-industrial parks, environmental justice, ecosystem management, recycling, watershed planning, agriculture, biodiversity, lifestyles, green buildings, energy conservation, pollution prevention, etc. Most sustainable community efforts try to address a range of such issues, recognizing the complexity and range of issues that need to be addressed in evolving to sustainability.

---

[4]"An eco-industrial park is a community of manufacturing and service businesses seeking enhanced environmental and economic performance through collaboration in managing environmental and resource issues including energy, water, and materials. By working together, the community of businesses seeks a collective benefit that is greater than the sum of individual benefits each company would realize if it optimized its individual performance." The President's Council on Sustainable Development, *Eco-Efficiency Task Force Report*, 1996, Appendix B4, p. 4.

An eco-industrial park (EIP) is also called an ecological industrial park .

To address such issues, communities may focus on education, technology development and implementation, and changing practices and behaviors of individuals, government, and/or businesses. Again, communities recognize that creating sustainability is difficult and will require a range of mechanisms and actions to be successful.

Another key element of such activities is the fact that community members work together often forming unique partnerships of individuals, community environmental groups, industry and businesses, academia, and local, state, and federal governments. Most of these communities feel that only through the combined skills and cooperative effort of every segment of the community can they become truly sustainable, especially given the unique and difficult problems that our communities face.

Chapter Three

ELEMENTS OF SUSTAINABLE COMMUNITIES

To better understand the relationship between sustainable community and P2 activities, it is important to understand how communities develop and implement their sustainability projects. This chapter presents an illustrative process for developing a sustainable community and describes two organizational concepts, illustrating them with examples from two communities.

PROCESS OF DEVELOPING A SUSTAINABLE COMMUNITY

Communities develop sustainability initiatives in many different ways. However, to illustrate this process, a sample of some of the most common steps is discussed in this chapter.

Below are seven procedures that communities often go through as they develop sustainable community efforts:

1. Developing ongoing governance structure for the sustainable community efforts;

2. Creating a sustainable community vision;

3. Setting goals and objectives along with indicators;

4. Developing sustainability guiding principles;

5. Designing and prioritizing potential activities;

6. Choosing and implementing activities; and

7. Evaluating progress and revising activities accordingly.

Each of these seven steps for this sample process of developing a sustainable community is briefly discussed.

Developing an Ongoing Governance Structure

Many sustainability efforts are started by enthusiastic individuals or organizations who want to help their community and environment. Such individuals or groups help motivate other members of the community to participate in the process. Often the process begins with a core group of volunteers and organizations meeting in a committee or workshop fashion. The group begins to organize a structure for the ongoing sustainable community effort, such as a steering committee that meets regularly and is open to the public. As the effort progresses, special subcommittees or task forces are created to develop and implement specific projects.

Creating a Vision

As a common first step, the sustainable community committee or group will first develop a vision for their sustainable community. This process typically includes reaching out to a wide range and large number of community stakeholders to help in developing the community vision. In developing this vision, community members often are asked by the sustainable community group questions such as: What does sustainability mean for my community or what do I want my community to look like in 20, 50, or 100 years? This development process frequently includes many discussions, public forums, and consensus building to create a common community vision. In this vision-making process, communities often create their own unique definitions of sustainability, as will be illustrated in Chapter Five with the City of Seattle's sustainable community effort.

Setting Goals and Objectives

Next, the group defines goals and objectives for their sustainable community and develops specific indicators to measure progress toward the community goals. Such a process may be time consuming, especially when it includes many different stakeholders and attempts to build community consensus. For instance, an indicators development project in Seattle took over three years. Seattle-area volunteers spent thousands of hours designing and researching the integrated "report card" on long-term trends in their region.

Developing Guiding Principles

Some communities also develop sustainability guiding principles to help individuals and organizations within their communities. For instance, Portland, Oregon, has developed sustainable city principles as guidelines for city elected officials and staff. Burlington, Vermont, has developed six principles of sustainable community development. Examples of these principles include: "Encourage economic self-sufficiency through local ownership and the maximum use of local resources"; "Equalize the benefits and burdens of growth"; and "Protect and preserve fragile environmental resources."[1]

Choosing and Implementing Activities

Once the sustainable community group has defined its vision, principles, goals, and objectives, it develops and prioritizes specific projects and actions to meet its goals and work toward the vision. Often the committee or subcommittee and/or task forces meet and brainstorm to generate ideas and analyze and discuss them. Key issues discussed include political and economic feasibility and resources available for implementation. After this discussion and analysis process, the ideas are prioritized for implementation. Then the community begins to choose which ones to implement and how to implement them. Some of the larger longer-term activities may require generating outside support and interest. Such a need occurs frequently when developing an eco-industrial park, as in Northampton County, Virginia, which attracted businesses to participate in its Sustainable Technologies Industrial Park. Short-term and low-cost projects may be started immediately, such as holding an educational meeting about home sustainability practices for local residents.

---

[1]The President's Council on Sustainable Development, *Sustainable Communities Task Force Report*, Final Draft, October 1996, p. 47.

Evaluating Progress and Revising Activities

Communities evaluate their progress and revise activities accordingly. This evaluation and revision step is especially important since sustainability is an evolutionary process. Some have criticized sustainable community activities because some communities have underemphasized the importance of measuring the actual effect of their activities. It is important to include a program evaluation process within such activities to measure the effectiveness of the program and to make necessary changes to improve it.

Not all sustainability processes happen this way; each community has unique elements in its process. This sample was presented to illustrate the general process that communities go through in developing sustainability efforts.

ORGANIZING FOR SUSTAINABILITY

How communities organize themselves for sustainability and how they organize their sustainability issues are both important parts of how sustainable communities develop. Communities tend to organize their functional structures and activities around sustainability issues. Specifically, they organize to address the economic, social, and environmental issues that are most pressing or most highly valued in their community. Many times they also address governance and management issues, such as fairness in their community, fairness in their sustainabilty process, and basic management logistics for the process. Integrating these issues is key, since communities are trying to address their problems in a more holistic and integrated fashion.

Many communities also organize their activities around basic community elements. These elements refer to the five functional and physical components that are the basis for our modern communities. Major community elements include the built environment, transportation, energy, water and wastes, and flora and fauna.[2] "Built environment" refers to buildings, such as residential, businesses, and

---

[2]These community elements were originally discussed by Jim Waddell and the author based on his 1995 NSTC draft white paper called "Reinventing the Urban Environment: The Role of Science and Technology."

other structures, and issues related to such structures. Issues addressed in this area include building materials, safe and affordable housing, and urban design. Transportation includes issues related to mobility and access to transportation. Water and waste includes issues such as drinking water, waste water, solid waste, and hazardous waste management. Flora and fauna refers to issues regarding natural resources and habitat such as green spaces, parks, species protection, agriculture, habitat restoration, and ecosystem management. Many communities try to address these elements in their organizational structure and activities. Again, in addressing these elements most communities consider the environment, economic issues, and social aspects and how they are interrelated.

This functional approach based on community elements is important for assessing the comprehensiveness of a sustainability activity. Some activities address one or two areas; others are more comprehensive and address all five. This structure also illustrates some of the confusion around the definition of sustainability and overuse of the term. If a project focuses only on energy issues, is it truly a sustainable community effort or just an energy activity? Such a judgment falls outside the scope of this report. However, it is important to be aware of such issues when thinking about the relationship between community activities that are called "sustainable" and P2.

In practice, most communities combine the issue and functional approaches. To illustrate this combination of such approaches, consider two different community organization examples: EcoVillage at Ithaca Guidelines for Development, and the Civic Forums in Cambridge, Massachusetts.

EcoVillage at Ithaca

EcoVillage at Ithaca created its Guidelines for Development over the course of nine months with input from over 100 people. These ideas are meant to be taken as guidelines rather than specific requirements. The Guidelines for Development were written for the following ten areas:

1. Residential neighborhood;
2. Village Center complex;

3. Agriculture;

4. Transportation and circulation;

5. Natural resources and recreation;

6. Water and wastewater;

7. Solid waste;

8. Energy;

9. Building materials; and

10. Social elements.[3]

The focus areas of these guidelines address all five of the major community elements as well important social elements of the community, including the Village Center. The guidelines focus on practical goals and objectives, such as the goal, "To maximize open space" and the objective, "Neighborhoods will surround an open, vehicle-free village green." Most of the guidelines are focused around the specific functional elements of the community that is being built.

Cambridge Civic Forums

The second example is from Cambridge, Massachusetts. The Cambridge Civic Forums are a joint project of the Center for Civic Networking, the Cambridge Center for Adult Education, the Cambridge Multicultural Arts Center, and the Sustainable Cambridge Coalition. The Civic Forums bring together Cambridge citizens to envision a healthy sustainable future for their community. In the forums, community members attempt to engage in a constructive dialogue, collaborate on defining a common vision, and participate in generating an action plan for the city's future. The Civic Forums have been organized around seven areas of conversation. These seven areas are:

---

[3]For more information, see EcoVillage at Ithaca, New York, WWW page: http://www.cfe.cornell.edu/ecovillage/.

1. Ecology;

2. The built environment;

3. Health and well-being;

4. Education and training;

5. Business and employment;

6. Social justice and governance; and

7. Arts and transcendent values.[4]

This example illustrates how the City of Cambridge focuses on a wide range of social, economic, and environmental issues in its discussions about the future. It places a great emphasis on social issues, such as justice, health, and the arts, in its process. For instance, health and well-being issues include citizens' physical well-being, which also may include mental issues such as stress and anxiety, health services delivery issues, and community access issues.

These two examples illustrate how each community takes its own approach to organizing environmental, social, and economic issues. The EcoVillage at Ithaca organizers have placed a greater emphasis on the practical functional elements of the community in providing their community guidelines, while Cambridge Civic Forums are organized around broader social and philosophical community issues. These differences also make sense given the nature of these two different sustainable community efforts: EcoVillage at Ithaca and its guidelines are focused on implementation (i.e., building a new neighborhood), whereas Cambridge Civic Forums are currently focused on a community visioning and planning process. An effort focused on the planning and visioning process may require a different structure from an effort focused more on implementation of specific projects, especially projects that focus more on technological and infrastructure changes. Note that if an effort's focus changes and evolves, such as moving from a visioning process to an implementation process, the organizational structure may also evolve.

---

[4]For more information on the Cambridge Civic Forums, see its WWW page: http://civic.net/cambridge_civic_network/ccf/ccf.html.

This fundamental point about differences in approach may seem frequently repeated, but one should remember that sustainable community efforts are unique, because each community's interest, goals, objectives, problems, members, and physical location are unique. Understanding this uniqueness means that the type of opportunity for P2 practitioners varies as well.

Chapter Four

RESOURCES FOR SUSTAINABILITY EFFORTS

Two important aspects of sustainable community projects are the range and source of resources. Many types of resources are provided to communities to aid in putting sustainability ideas into action. Resources include information, funding, man-hours, materials, expertise, and labor. Political, managerial, and community commitment and support are also important resources that many community efforts receive.

Where do communities obtain information, funding, and other support for their sustainability ideas? Resources are available from many different sources including federal, state, and local governments; industry; professional associations; universities; and non-governmental organizations (NGOs). This chapter provides examples of how each of these sources has supported sustainability efforts. The bibliography contains more specific examples for such resources, including points of contact (POC), phone numbers, and WWW addresses. A wealth of these resources are available; this document provides only a sample.

FEDERAL GOVERNMENT

The federal government has acknowledged the importance of sustainable community efforts by supporting them at various levels. At the highest level, the President of the United States established the President's Council on Sustainable Development (PCSD) by Executive Order on June 29, 1993. The PCSD's mission was to develop and recommend to the President a national sustainable development action strategy, to develop an annual Presidential Honors Program recognizing outstanding achievements in sustainable development, and to raise public awareness about sustainability. The 25-member council was a unique partnership of leaders from industry, government, environmental, labor, and civil rights organizations. The council organized eight task forces to address different issues related to sustainability:

1. Eco-efficiency;

2. Energy and transportation;

3. Natural resources management and protection;

4. Population and consumption;

5. Principles, goals, and definitions;

6. Public linkage, dialogue, and education;

7. Sustainable agriculture; and

8. Sustainable communities.

During 1996, the PCSD and task forces released their policy recommendations in a series of reports, which are useful references about sustainable community issues and activities.[1] For example, the report "Education for Sustainability: An Agenda for Action," provides useful recommendations about how every stakeholder can become involved in sustainability education. The PCSD also has been facilitating the development of other resources for sustainable community efforts, such as providing an inventory of sustainable development resources within the federal government.

In the process of developing the National Environmental Technology Strategy (NETS), the many different stakeholders (i.e., the U.S. government, industry, academia, and community groups) recognized how important sustainable community activities are for promoting and implementing environmental technologies and achieving na-

---

[1]For more information about the PCSD and its reports, contact the PCSD at 202-408-5296 or see its WWW page: http://www.whitehouse.gov/PCSD. Also, see the bibliography at the end of this report.

tional sustainability.[2] NETS set the following goal for sustainable communities:

> Develop and implement sustainability plans in many U.S. communities and make significant progress toward achieving sustainable communities over the next 25 years, increasing the quality of urban, suburban, and rural life and reducing our use of energy and natural resources.[3]

The federal government is currently in the process of implementing this strategy. Specifically, federal agencies are assisting communities so they can more successfully integrate the development and use of environmental technologies into their sustainability plans and actions.

The federal government has extensive sustainability resources within many different agencies including

- The U.S. Environmental Protection Agency (EPA);

- The Department of Energy (DOE);

- The Department of Commerce National Oceanic and Atmospheric Administration (NOAA);

- The United States Department of Agriculture (USDA); and

- The Department of the Interior (DOI).

Their aid to community sustainability efforts includes seed money, labor, expertise, and information.

EPA created the Office of Sustainable Ecosystems and Communities (OSEC) within EPA's Office of Policy, Planning and Evaluation, to assist local community sustainability efforts. Through OSEC and other parts of the agency, EPA has increased emphasis on place-based management for local communities. EPA is helping enable

---

[2]Sustainable communities were an important theme emerging from the many stakeholder events held to develop this strategy. Beth Lachman, Robert Lempert, Susan Resetar, and Thomas Anderson, *Technology for a Sustainable Future, Ideas: A Summary of Workshop Discussions*, RAND, RP-417, 1995.

[3]*Bridge to a Sustainable Future: National Environmental Technology Strategy*, Government Printing Office, Washington, D.C., April 1995, p. 53.

community-based environmental protection (CBEP) projects that build on sustainability principles. EPA's Urban and Economic Development Division is also assisting communities with growth and development issues related to sustainability.

DOE has helped sponsor many sustainability efforts with extensive energy and technology expertise. Many DOE labs have worked with communities in their region as well as across the country to help develop sustainability projects. For instance, DOE's Office of Energy Efficiency and Renewable Energy has been active in helping natural disaster victims in sustainable redevelopment by providing design assistance teams in collaboration with state agencies such as the Illinois Department of Natural Resources, NGOs, and other organizations. One such project was helping Valmeyer, Illinois, relocate and rebuild after it was devastated by a flood. DOE has also created a Center of Excellence for Sustainable Development to help assist community efforts.

The Department of Commerce (DOC) also supports sustainable community activities, such as some of its NOAA programs. For example, NOAA's Coastal Zone Management Program has helped fund and provided technical support to coastal sustainable community activities, such as the Northampton County, Virginia, initiative. Curry County, Oregon, a rural community whose economy has been based on logging and fishing, has a Sustainable Nature-Based Tourism Project to design, build, and implement a sustainable economic sector. One of its pilot projects involves tourists helping to restore stream habitat for salmon. This sustainable community effort received some initial funding from the federal government through a NOAA coastal program.

The USDA is working with university researchers, communities, and NGOs to help develop and implement more sustainable agriculture practices, which help increase farmer income and minimize agricultural effects. For example, in the Chesapeake Bay area, USDA helps to develop and implement practices that reduce nutrient runoff, which helps protect the bay.

The Department of Interior also assists sustainable community activities. For example, the National Park Service's Presidio National Park is trying to educate the public about sustainability in its effort to become a Center for Sustainability. The Federal Geographic Data Committee (FGDC), an interagency committee chaired by the Secretary of the Interior with staff support from the United States Geological Survey (USGS), is leading the development of the National Spatial Data Infrastructure (NSDI). The NSDI vision facilitates the availability of geospatial data locally, nationally, and globally to aid in economic growth, environmental stability, and social progress. The FGDC coordinates federal geographic data activities and provides leadership for the NSDI in partnership with state and local governments, academia, the private sector, and others. Activities to establish the NSDI include developing standards for geographic data, building an electronic clearinghouse to help find and access spatial data, and developing a framework of basic spatial data to aid in integrating geographic data. The implementation of the NSDI will help provide data to meet the decisionmaking and scientific needs of sustainability, by improving data sharing, reducing redundant data collection, and facilitating and building community-based partnerships to address problems and issues across common pieces of geography.

STATE GOVERNMENTS

State governments also provide leadership and resources for sustainability activities. For instance, Minnesota has developed a strategic plan for sustainable development and is actively supporting and promoting sustainability activities. The main goals of the state's sustainability effort, called the Minnesota Sustainable Development Initiative, are "sustaining Minnesota's economy, ecosystems, and communities, educating its citizens and organizing its institutions for sustainable development." This initiative includes six strategic directions for achieving these goals:

1. Aligning Minnesota's economic incentives and goals;

2. Understanding what is environmentally sustainable;

3. Integrating natural resources management;

4. Advancing sustainable land use and community development policies;

5. Asking government to take the first steps; and

6. Focusing research on sustainable development issues.[4]

Minnesota's state environmental agencies' staff members assist local governments and communities in developing and implementing sustainable community projects. For instance, the Minnesota Office of Environmental Assistance (OEA) has a sustainable communities team that helps public-private coalitions promote sustainable development in their communities by offering educational and training materials, seed money, conferences, and other resources. OEA and other state agencies also sponsored a state sustainable development conference in October 1996, which was attended by over 600 people.

Florida has developed an Ecosystem Management Plan, which builds on sustainability, and has created a Governor's Commission for a Sustainable South Florida. The 42-person commission consists of state and regional agencies and legislative, business, local government, tribal, public interest, and nonvoting federal members. This commission is developing strategies and actions for making South Florida more sustainable. Its efforts include improving intergovernmental coordination and more sustainable allocation of natural resources in urban and rural areas, including promoting sustainability within the Everglades ecosystem.

Many states are exploring the concepts of sustainable development and starting to provide statewide leadership and develop statewide initiatives. The PCSD's *Sustainable Communities Task Force Report* provides a list of statewide contacts for over a dozen states.[5]

LOCAL GOVERNMENTS

Many local governments also provide leadership and resources. Individual community governments, such as Northampton County, Virginia, the City of Seattle, and the City of Chattanooga, discussed throughout this report, actively support sustainable community projects. Another local government example is Metro-Dade County,

---

[4] *Challenge for a Sustainable Minnesota: A Minnesota Strategic Plan for Sustainable Development*, Minnesota Sustainable Development Initiative, Minnesota Environmental Quality Board, Public Review Draft, July 1995.

[5] The President's Council on Sustainable Development, *Sustainable Communities Task Force Report*, Final Draft, October 1996, Appendix D, pp. 230–233.

Florida. This county has a range of sustainable programs, including helping to develop and build a more resource-efficient community, called Jordan Commons.

Steele County, Minnesota, has a "Green Source 2020" project focused on "sustaining our community through environmental awareness and actions."[6] This project, funded by the Minnesota Office of Environmental Assistance and Steele County Environmental Services, is helping to educate farmers and other community citizens about why sustainability is important and what they can do to help.

The National Association of Counties (NACo) and the United States Conference of Mayors (USCM) has a new Joint Center for Sustainable Communities. The Joint Center "will foster sustainable communities by providing local officials with advice, information, and financial support" through a range of programs. These programs include

- Sustainable community grants;
- Development of metropolitan compacts to create multijurisdictional partnerships for addressing regional issues;
- Sustainable community awards;
- Leadership training;
- A peer exchange program to match experienced officials with other jurisdictions that need assistance;
- Development of a catalogue of needed tools;
- Information clearinghouse;
- Public policy forums; and
- National education.[7]

This Joint Center should be a useful resource for local communities in their sustainability activities.

---

[6]"Green Source 2020," brochure from Steele County Environmental Services.

[7]"Joint Center for Sustainable Communities," informational flyer. For more information contact the Joint Center for Sustainable Communities through Jerry McNeil, Director, Community Services Division, NACo, 202-942-4237, and Dave Gatton, Senior Environmental Advisor, USCM, 202-293-7330.

INDUSTRY AND PROFESSIONAL ASSOCIATIONS

Industry and professional associations are also active in helping to develop and implement sustainable community projects. For example, industries are partnering in eco-industrial park activities. Another interesting industry example is Integrated Building and Construction Solutions, Inc. (IBACOS). In Pittsburgh, IBACOS serves as a successful model where private entities in partnership with the federal government are developing, testing, and commercializing innovative housing products and systems that are more environmentally friendly. For instance, IBACOS homes contain more energy efficient technologies and carpets and roof tiles made out of recycled plastics. These homes, which are quick to build, top quality, affordable, and adaptable, can help communities develop more sustainable residential building practices.

During fall 1995, the American Institute of Architects (AIA) helped organize and sponsor a series of three-day intensive workshops, called Environmental Design Charrettes, focused on developing and implementing community sustainability projects. These AIA communities included Bridgeport, Connecticut; Fort Collins, Colorado; Greensboro, North Carolina; Independence, Missouri; Kane'ohe, Hawaii; Kansas City, Missouri; Milwaukee, Wisconsin; Minneapolis, Minnesota; New Bedford, Massachusetts; Newton/Waltham, Massachusetts; San Antonio, Texas; San Francisco, California; Santa Barbara, California; Santa Monica, California; and Waterloo, Iowa.

The American Association of Engineering Societies (AAES) is another example of a professional society helping to promote sustainability activities. AAES facilitates integrating sustainability principles and practices into engineering education, training, and activities. For example, it has published "The Role of Engineering in Sustainable Development" as a basic primer on sustainability for engineering professionals. The Civil Engineering Research Foundation (CERF) also supports sustainability activities, such as addressing the linkage of infrastructure design and future sustainability.

UNIVERSITIES

Universities provide technical assistance, education, and research and development needed for sustainability. For instance, the Center for Sustainability at the University of Washington has assisted Seattle and other communities. The Center for Sustainability also has an extensive web site that includes tutorials on sustainability issues such as "The three E's: Ecology, Economy, Equity."[8] The Center for Sustainable Development at Georgia Institute of Technology has developed and tested a curriculum on sustainable development for engineering undergraduate students. Cornell University's Center for the Environment has been working with the Baltimore Development Corporation in the planning and implementation of the Fairfield Ecological Industrial Park in Baltimore, Maryland. The Center for Urban Transportation Research at the University of South Florida is undertaking the State Transportation Policy Initiative, which is reevaluating the way transportation infrastructure and services are planned and developed in Florida. This study includes research related to transportation, land use, and sustainability. The National Pollution Prevention Center for Higher Education at the University of Michigan provides education and conducts research in industrial ecology[9] and other areas that are important for developing and implementing more sustainable practices. Industrial ecology research is especially important for eco-industrial park activities.

Universities themselves are also trying to become more sustainable. George Washington University, for instance, has a Green University Initiative, in which it is trying to implement sustainable practices in all aspects of George Washington University operations and community life.

NON-GOVERNMENTAL ORGANIZATIONS

NGOs have also been active in sustainable community projects. These organizations may work directly with communities on sus-

---

[8]To access this site, see: http://weber.u.washington.edu/~common/epa/contents/ session6.html.

[9]Industrial ecology refers to "a closed-loop system in which resources and energy flow into production processes and excess materials are put back into the loop so that little or no waste is generated. Products used by consumers flow back into production loops through recycling to recover resources. Ideally, loops are closed within a factory, among industries in a region, and within national and global economies." *Technology for a Sustainable Future: A Framework for Action*, Government Printing Office, Washington, D.C., 1994, p. 54.

tainability projects, publish information about success stories, and even develop educational curriculum for the schools. Examples of such organizations include Renew America, The Nature Conservancy, Environmental Defense Fund, The Izaak Walton League of America, The Green Institute, CONCERN, Inc., and Public Technology, Inc.

Each year Renew America identifies, verifies, and promotes examples of successful environmental programs. Its annual "Environmental Success Index" includes sustainable development examples.

The Nature Conservancy has started working with local communities in "ecologically compatible development" based on sustainability. In 1995, its national office created the Center for Compatible Economic Development to explore the use of market forces and economic development as tools for biodiversity conservation. The Virginia Chapter has helped to create strategic visions for ecologically compatible development for eleven counties in Southwest Virginia and eastern Tennessee.[10]

The Environmental Defense Fund (EDF), a nonprofit environmental research and advocacy group, has also been developing resources for sustainability projects. EDF has created a tool kit on sustainability for communities based on the work of its Pollution Prevention Alliance. Its *Environmental Sustainability Kit* emphasizes P2 and is a guide to help communities start sustainability initiatives.[11]

The Izaak Walton League of America, a national nonprofit conservation organization, provides educational materials related to sustainability. This organizations has developed a supplementary environmental education mini-curriculum for grades nine through twelve called *Community Sustainability.*[12]

---

[10]"Virginia Chapter News," *The Nature Conservancy,* Spring 1996.

[11]*Environmental Sustainability Kit,* prepared by the Pollution Prevention Alliance, Environmental Defense Fund, October 1996. For more information, contact Meena Palaniappan at 202-387-3500.

[12]Benedict J. Hren and Diane M. Hren, *Community Sustainability: A Mini-Curriculum for Grades 9–12,* The Izaak Walton League of America, 1996. The Izaak Walton League of America can be contacted at 301-548-0150.

The Green Institute is a nonprofit organization that grew out of a grassroots neighborhood effort to stop construction of a major garbage transfer station in the inner-city Phillips neighborhood of Minneapolis, Minnesota. This organization is "dedicated to creating new models of sustainable environmental and community revitalization." The Green Institute has helped sponsor a study about eco-industrial parks and publishes a quarterly newsletter to provide a forum for community issues of environmental and economic sustainability.[13]

CONCERN, Inc., is a nonprofit environmental group dedicated to improving the quality of life in communities. This organization offers a list of resources for sustainability and other materials including case studies, workbooks, manuals, audio-visuals, and electronic sources of information. CONCERN is also trying to build a national database of sustainable community projects to foster networking and collaboration.[14]

Public Technology, Inc. (PTI) is a nonprofit technology organization of the National League of Cities (NLC), the National Association of Counties (NACo), and the International City/County Management Association (ICMA). This organization helps provide sustainability information for local governments in areas such as transportation and building construction.

These examples illustrate that many types of resources from many sources are available to help support sustainable community efforts. Such sustainability resources can also be used for P2 activities, which will be discussed in Chapter Six. For more information on these and other organizations and the type of resources they have provided to sustainable community efforts, see the annotated bibliography at the end of this report.

---

[13]For more information, contact The Green Institute at 612-874-1148.

[14]CONCERN, Inc., can be contacted at 202-328-8160.

Chapter Five

SUSTAINABLE COMMUNITY EXAMPLES

This chapter provides examples of community sustainability projects. It begins by providing a broad geographical sampling of projects under way in various communities in the United States. It follows with detailed descriptions of projects in four communities: Northampton County, Virginia; Seattle, Washington; EcoVillage at Ithaca, New York; and Presidio National Park, San Francisco, California.

A GEOGRAPHICAL SAMPLE OF SUSTAINABLE COMMUNITY PROJECTS

There are hundreds of examples of sustainable community projects across the United States. Such projects occur in all types of communities—in large, medium, and small cities; in towns; in counties; and in rural communities. Table 1 shows the diversity of the communities by listing 30 communities across the United States that have done some sort of sustainability project.

This sample was selected from a range of sources including the PCSD community case study list, the AIA environmental design charrette projects focused on sustainability, studies by the Center for Sustainability at the University of Washington, and examples from various workshops and conferences held to help develop and implement the National Environmental Technology Strategy. Many other examples can be found in the bibliography at the end of this report.

Table 1

Examples of Communities with Sustainability Projects

Arlington, VA	New Haven, CT
Atlanta, GA	New York, NY
Baltimore, MD	Northampton County, VA
Brownsville, TX	Olympia, WA
Charlottesville, VA	Pattonsburg, MO
Chattanooga, TN	Portland, OR
Chicago, IL	Presidio Natl.Park, CA
Cleveland, OH	San Francisco, CA
Curry County, OR	San Jose, CA
Haymount, VA	Santa Monica, CA
Henryetta, OK	Sarasota, FL
Ithaca, NY	Seattle, WA
Los Angeles/Pico Union, CA	Steele County, MN
Minneapolis, MN	Waterloo, IA
New Bedford, MA	Zuni, NM

These communities use different definitions of sustainable community. Some also call their efforts by a different name, such as an ecovillage or a sustainable development project. However, most of these efforts share the basic principles of a sustainable community, namely, trying to take a long-term systems approach to community problems by addressing environmental, economic, and social issues in an integrated manner. It should be noted that no attempt has been made to evaluate their effectiveness or their current status, since that is outside the scope of this report. Some of these community projects may even have ended, as has happened with the Arlington Community Sustainability Network. Those interested should contact the community directly or see the references at the end of this report to learn the current status of these activities.

FOUR COMMUNITY EXAMPLES

The remainder of this chapter presents four detailed examples of sustainable community projects. These examples were chosen to reflect the communities and range of activities and issues that sustainability efforts address, from protecting birding habitat to controlling urban sprawl, from building a new neighborhood to creating eco-industrial parks. The communities and projects are:

Northampton County, Virginia, a rural county with a sustainable economic development effort.

City of Seattle, a comprehensive initiative to address its urban problems including urban sprawl.

Ithaca, New York, a project to develop a new more sustainable neighborhood on previously undeveloped land.

Presidio National Park, an effort to try to make the park into a showcase for sustainability and sustainable practices.

These efforts are currently being implemented. Most have shown some initial success, but it remains to be seen how successful they will be in the long term.

Northampton County, Virginia

Northampton County, Virginia, is often cited as a model of small-town and rural sustainable development. Northampton County is the southernmost county on Virginia's Eastern Shore, forming the gateway to the Chesapeake Bay. The county is rich in natural and cultural assets including beaches, marshes, barrier islands, tidal creeks, woodlands, historic villages, and farms. It includes a diverse habitat for over 260 species of birds and countless other fish and wildlife species. The county also has been one of the poorest in Virginia. In 1991 the Virginia Coastal Resources Management Program of the Virginia Department of Environmental Quality (DEQ) approached the county with a four-year match-free grant proposal, a Special Area Management Plan (SAMP) for sustainable development, to create enforceable policies to protect coastal habitat and promote economic development. A partnership of federal, state, and local governments was formed. With a $1 million grant from NOAA under the Coastal Zone Management Act, the Virginia Coastal Program hired a local project coordinator and a citizens' Sustainable Development Task Force was created. The task force held a series of community meetings. Northampton County's Board of Supervisors also supported this effort.

This community task force created a Sustainable Development Action Strategy based on the Special Area Management Plan. This strategy targets six industry areas for sustainable development and links each with key asset protection policies. These targets are to develop:

1. The heritage tourism industry while protecting natural and cultural assets.

2. Seafood and aquaculture industries while protecting water quality.

3. New industries, including an eco-industrial park, while protecting sense of place, quality of life, and the groundwater.

4. The agriculture industry while protecting productive land, including sensitive habitats.

5. Arts, crafts, and local product industries while preserving culturally diverse authentic communities.

6. Research and education facilities while protecting natural and cultural systems.

Northampton County has already begun implementing these projects. This initiative has shown some initial success, and the group continues to leverage resources for its project implementation. Additional support and resources have been acquired from the Department of Transportation, the Economic Development Administration, the U.S. Department of Agriculture, the U.S. Fish and Wildlife Service, the Environmental Protection Agency, and industry.

The following two examples illustrate the project's progress. The first illustrates how the Special Area Management Plan developed bird-watching tourism while protecting habitat, and the second focuses on the Port of Cape Charles Sustainable Technologies Industrial Park (STIP).

Beginning in the fall of 1991, the Virginia Coastal Program contracted with various agencies and organizations to research bird habitat requirements in the area, particularly neotropical migratory songbirds and colonial waterbirds. In 1993, the Virginia Coastal Program initiated the annual Eastern Shore Birding Festival. The Eastern Shore Chamber of Commerce now organizes the event, which is funded largely through the SAMP for sustainable development and is put on through the efforts of many federal, state, and local agencies and private citizens. The festival celebrates the annual fall migration of songbirds, raptors, shorebirds, and other birds. Over 160 species are usually seen during the Festival weekend and several hundred thousand dollars are brought in by the birdwatchers.

The Port of Cape Charles Sustainable Technologies Industrial Park (STIP) is an eco-industrial park project. Funded by a unique partnership of federal, state, private, and county investments, the STIP is starting to attract businesses committed to profitability, the environment, and the community. The park will incorporate local enterprises as well as new industry as it tries to create more sustainable products and production practices. The STIP will attempt to demonstrate advanced facilities in resource efficiency and pollution prevention and model symbiotic relationships among industrial processes. STIP's first tenant—a manufacturer of photovoltaic energy equipment—is already in place.

Through many different project activities and its ability to leverage support and resources from many different stakeholders and sources, Northampton County's sustainability effort illustrates how rural communities and small towns can make progress toward sustainability.

Seattle, Washington

Seattle was one of the first U.S. cities to explicitly incorporate sustainability concepts as an organizing principle for community planning and development. As defined by the volunteer civic organization Sustainable Seattle, "sustainability" here refers to the "the long-term social, economic, and environmental health of our community." Seattle refined its definition in two ways:

1. "Sustainability-enhancing decisionmaking" refers to holistic and long-term choices.

2. A "sustainable city" is one that "thrives without compromising the ability of future generations to meet their needs."

An important part of Seattle's "sustainable city" definition is the concept of the city as a system within a system—a web of social, economic, and ecological phenomena operating within a similar but larger regional, national, and global system. Neighborhoods must prosper within the web of the city. Sustainability-enhancing decisionmaking (from public policy to individual lifestyles) considers the effects that decisions are likely to have on the entire system (i.e., economic, social, and environmental issues) and on future generations.

Since 1990, many new city policies, plans, programs, and redevelopment projects have included sustainability. For instance, the Seattle Comprehensive Plan hopes to reduce urban sprawl and traffic congestion by increasing the density of jobs, housing, and amenities around "Urban Village" centers while maintaining the unique character of individual neighborhoods. This Comprehensive Plan's development was mandated by the Washington State Growth Management Act. Furthermore, over 30 Seattle neighborhoods are nvolved in the Neighborhood Planning Project, a follow-up project to the Comprehensive Plan. This project is a two- to four-year planning process to design plans consistent with the city's overall objective of sustainability while also meeting neighborhoods' special needs.

Seattle has also been working with industry in its sustainability efforts. For example, Boeing and the City of Seattle have agreed to use waste heat from a new sewer trunk line to provide heat for the company's major assembly facilities, saving on the cost of both heating equipment and fuel.

Seattle is also noted for its ongoing development of sustainability indicators—quality-of-life metrics that reflect economic, ecological, social, and cultural health. For example, the 1995 metrics focused on environmental indicators related to wetlands, biodiversity, wild salmon, air quality, pedestrian-friendly streets, open space in Urban Villages, impervious surfaces, and soil erosion. The 1995 metrics for population and resources focused on population, pollution prevention and renewable resource use, solid waste generated and recycled, residential water consumption, vehicle miles traveled and fuel consumption, and farm acreage. Such metrics will be used to evaluate the effectiveness of the various programs and public expenditures toward achieving sustainability.

Seattle has built a substantial collaborative process with government and private leadership. The mayor and some members of the city council and King County Council have publicly embraced sustainability. The mayor's Environmental Action Agenda created a more "holistic" management strategy for achieving key environmental priorities defined by community consensus. This agenda also helped initiate projects to integrate environmental, economic, and social goals. Many grassroots citizens' groups and nonprofit institutions and universities also have helped in Seattle's activities, including researchers and educators at the Northwest Policy Center; the Center for Sustainability Communities (Cascadia Community and Environment Institute); and the Institute for Environmental Studies at the University of Washington and Seattle University. EPA Region X has also been supportive of Seattle's sustainability activities.

Seattle's sustainability program has experienced growing pains and mixed success. Sustainability is especially difficult when it attempts to change individual behaviors, such as trying to decrease single-occupancy vehicle driving and to solve related urban sprawl issues. Seattle found that "many new programs and policies that would have the effect of promoting more sustainable behavior in the region have met with stiff opposition. Often, the object at the center of the conflict is the private automobile."[1] Because of such opposition, Seattle reworked its Comprehensive Plan, somewhat weakening and simplifying it while retaining the commitment to sustainability and the "Urban Village" strategy. Seattle learned from experience and continues to try to evolve toward sustainability, recognizing that becoming more sustainable is often a slow and incremental process.

Many of Seattle's most successful sustainability projects have been decentralized, grassroots efforts. For instance, city- and county-sponsored programs have successfully trained and deployed volunteers throughout the region to help teach individuals about more sustainable practices. These volunteers have included "Friends of Recycling," "Master Composters," and "Master Gardeners." Many small businesses are implementing more sustainable practices, from eco-retailers to bicycling carpet cleaners.

---

[1] *Sustainability in Seattle 1995, A Report to the President's Council on Sustainable Development*, A Joint Project by the Center for Sustainable Communities, Sustainable Seattle, and AtKisson & Associates, Inc., 1995, p. 11.

EcoVillage at Ithaca, New York

EcoVillage at Ithaca, New York, is another type of sustainable community initiative where members are trying to develop a new community from the ground up. Over five years ago, a grassroots group of citizens, with assistance from the Center for Religion, Ethics, and Social Policy at Cornell University, formed EcoVillage at Ithaca in Ithaca, New York. The group's goal is to create a model community of about 500 residents that will exemplify sustainable systems of living. Its completed project is supposed to be a working demonstration of a community that meets basic human needs such as shelter, food production, energy, social interaction, work, and recreation while preserving natural ecosystems.

With the help of donations and loans, the group purchased a 176-acre site less than two miles from downtown Ithaca. Through an envisioning retreat in 1991 and four land-use planning forums during 1992 and 1993, members of EcoVillage at Ithaca developed comprehensive plans for their new community. The process of developing the project included input from over 100 people including future residents, architects, landscape architects, students, professors, planners, ecologists, and energy experts. The group formed a plan to build five neighborhoods around a village green, while preserving at least 80 percent of the land as agricultural open space, woods, and wetlands.

EcoVillage at Ithaca's plan includes an integrated strategy for addressing issues such as transportation, land use, energy, water, waste water, solid wastes, agriculture, cultural and ethnic diversity, recreation, natural resources, building materials, education, research, and residential neighborhoods. For instance, the village is building a pedestrian-oriented, mixed-use multifamily development on less than 20 percent of the land while using most of the rest of the land for agriculture and natural areas. State-of-the-art permaculture techniques, including orcharding, agroforestry, and aquaculture, will be implemented to maximize the self-sufficiency of the village. Other plans include an on-site wastewater treatment via a natural marsh system, gray water recycling, and composting. To be highly energy-efficient, houses are being built with super-insulated passive-solar designs and shared hot water heating systems. A visitor center will be constructed, which will also support education and research activities. The program has already developed educational programs in ecology and agriculture for local youth.

A group of residents formed the EcoVillage CoHousing Cooperative, a separate legal entity that is creating cohousing neighborhoods on EcoVillage's land based on the Danish CoHousing model. Private, self-contained homes are being built in clusters around shared spaces, including a pedestrian path and a common house. The common house may include optional shared space such as a kitchen, dining room, laundry facility, workshops, guest rooms, and children and exercise areas. The first neighborhood was to have been built by the end of 1996 and was to include 15 duplexes clustered around a pedestrian courtyard. In developing this project, the EcoVillage Co-Housing Cooperative had to overcome some challenging zoning regulations.[2] To learn more about these and other implementation issues of the EcoVillage at Ithaca project, see the bibliography at the end of this report.

This example demonstrates how a small city with a grassroots effort can start to build a new village within the city to create a model for sustainable living.

Presidio National Park

Another sustainability initiative is the Presidio of San Francisco, a former Army base in the heart of San Francisco. It is now a National Historic Park operated by the National Park Service (NPS). However, the Presidio is a unique national park. Besides preserving and interpreting history and protecting the environment for millions of visitors to enjoy every year, this park is also trying to become a center for sustainability. The Presidio is developing and implementing projects to demonstrate more sustainable practices. Teaching about sustainability and transferring its sustainable practices to other communities are major goals of this initiative. The Presidio is developing spe-

---

[2]Many times sustainable community projects may need to overcome barriers in traditional government policy and regulations that encourage unsustainable practices or prohibit the type of innovation that sustainability projects are trying to test. Another example of such a barrier for eco-industrial parks is environmental regulations, such as permitting procedures, that hinder the free flow of certain waste maerials from one company's facility to be used as inputs at a different company's adjacent facility.

cial educational projects, such as special visitors' tours of Presidio grounds and sustainability projects, to teach visitors about sustainability.

In October 1995, in cooperation with the AIA, the Department of Energy, and the NPS, the Presidio held an environmental design charrette to develop sustainability projects for the Presidio. Over 100 people, including architects, environmental consultants, engineers, exhibit designers, members of the neighboring community, developers, students, and NPS personnel, spent three days developing demonstration projects. Their goal was to create a sense of community and to develop plans for specific sustainability projects at the Presidio. This community's members include federal and local government, private businesses, NGOs, and private citizens.

The demonstration projects were organized by six focus areas, with a team of volunteers working in each area before and after the charrette. The focus areas were:

1. Historic residential building rehabilitation;

2. Historic non-residential building rehabilitation;

3. Waste prevention;

4. Natural habitat preservation and restoration;

5. Transportation; and

6. Total site concerns.

Projects are currently being implemented in all areas. For instance, participants are trying to protect and enhance Mountain Lake, the only natural lake at the Presidio. This project includes educating the general public, and especially school children, in lake and riparian area ecology, hydrology, biology, and management. The transportation team's projects include acquiring electric transit vehicles, improving bike and pedestrian trails, and establishing information kiosks with educational exhibits. The waste prevention team is assisting the park in implementing source reduction projects in all operations and reclaiming construction debris for reuse in other areas of the park. Again, educational exhibits and tours will be a key part of the projects.

The park has many historic buildings, which are being rebuilt and thus pose special challenges because of their historic status. The two building rehabilitation teams have been designing special demonstration projects for rehabilitating historic buildings. These projects will be economical for the tenants, more resource-efficient and energy-efficient, and educational for the public.

The total site team helped facilitate a process for creating a sense of community for the various stakeholders involved with the Presidio. These stakeholders include workers, residents, neighbors, visitors, recreational users, and interested members of the general public. This community also includes private businesses, such as Burger King and golf course managers, NPS personnel, and military personnel and families who still live at the park. Other community members include NGOs that are tenants on the Presidio, such as the Tides Foundation, and those who have a special interest in it, such as local Sierra Club members. There is now a designated community center where regular meetings are held.

The Presidio teams hope that they can create sustainability models to be transferred to private and public communities worldwide, such as towns, cities, other national parks, and military bases that are being converted and reused.

These four examples illustrate ambitious plans for different sustainable community efforts. Each community has experienced some initial successes; however, it remains to be seen how successful they will be at meeting their longer-term sustainability goals. Hopefully, these efforts and other new sustainable community approaches will be successful in creating long-term healthy communities.

Next, this report discusses pollution prevention and explores the relationship between P2 activities and sustainable community activities.

Chapter Six

RELATIONSHIPS BETWEEN SUSTAINABLE COMMUNITY AND P2 ACTIVITIES

Thus far, this report has defined key terms and described the organization for and processes of sustainable community activities. This chapter outlines the relation between these activities and pollution prevention. It begins by defining P2 and describing the hierarchy of related activities, since different organizations and individuals may use slightly different definitions of P2. It then describes how sustainability initiatives incorporate P2 activities. Next, the chapter discusses the relevance of sustainable community activities for P2 activities. Finally, it provides some guidelines showing how P2 programs can take advantage of sustainable community activities and offers a list of specific steps for P2 practitioners to take.

DEFINITION OF POLLUTION PREVENTION

EPA's definition of pollution prevention follows the Pollution Prevention Act of 1990 and Executive Order 12856—Federal Compliance with Right-to-Know Laws and Pollution Prevention Requirements (August 3, 1993):

> any practice which reduces the amount of hazardous substance, pollutant, or contaminant entering any waste stream or otherwise released into the environment (including fugitive emissions) prior to recycling, treatment, or disposal; and any practice which reduces the hazards to public health and the environment associated with the release of such substances, pollutants, or contaminants.

This definition focuses on source reduction activities by referring to the use of materials, processes, or practices that eliminate or reduce the quantity of toxic wastes and the toxicity of those wastes at the source of generation, namely, activities prior to waste generation. Such activities include process efficiency improvements, material substitution, preventive maintenance, improved housekeeping, and inventory control. Besides including practices that eliminate the discharge of harmful wastes, this definition also includes practices that protect natural resources through conservation and efficiency. Pollution prevention also reduces the use of hazardous materials, energy, and water.

Many pollution prevention practitioners both within government and private industry have adopted what is called an environmental protection or environmental management hierarchy. This hierarchy presents options for managing waste in priority order: source reduction, recycling, treatment, and disposal. Whenever possible, individuals and organizations should first implement practices that reduce or eliminate wastes at the source. Source reduction is the highest priority because it reduces or eliminates wastes at the source of generation. Recycling is the next preferable option because it is the reuse or regeneration of materials and wastes into usable products. Treatment and disposal are considered last resort options. Definitions of this hierarchy may vary slightly from organization to organization.

Federal environmental regulations and EPA guidance documents use these definitions. State regulations also specifically define their definitions of pollution prevention and this hierarchy. Usually, states use EPA's definitions, such as in their state pollution prevention acts. However, states also may change the interpretation slightly in their legislation.

In practice, businesses and state and local governments have flexibility in what they label as P2 and what they implement as P2 activities. For example, some businesses and some local governments consider recycling to be pollution prevention, although technically it is not part of the official P2 definition. Another important gray area in implementing P2 activities is avoidance of environmental harm. Is an activity that helps reduce the loss of biodiversity, species, and/or habitat considered P2? Individuals and organizations would differ in their answer to this question, although many state and local governments do not currently include such a focus in their P2 activities. This flexibility in P2 activities actually allows for more opportunity to take advantage of sustainable community efforts.

Now that P2 has been defined and the reader understands how sustainable community activities are organized, what is the relationship between sustainable community and P2 activities? The next section begins to answer this question by explaining how sustainable communities use P2 as a tool in their sustainability projects.

HOW SUSTAINABLE COMMUNITY ACTIVITIES INCORPORATE P2

Many communities consider P2 as a building block for sustainability. Sustainable community efforts incorporate pollution prevention in their activities in different ways. Some communities explicitly mention P2 in their goals and objective. For example, EcoVillage at Ithaca has a solid waste goal focused on P2: "To reduce the amount of solid waste generated on-site." In Seattle, sustainability indicators include metrics for pollution prevention and renewable resource use. P2 is considered an important indicator to help measure progress toward sustainability.

Pollution prevention is almost always a major element of specific project design, development, and implementation. For instance, Chattanooga, Tennessee; Baltimore, Maryland; Northampton County, Virginia; Brownsville, Texas; and other community efforts to develop eco-industrial parks include elements focused on P2 to strive for zero emissions from their facilities. Elements of the eco-industrial park approach "include new or retrofitted design of park infrastructure and plants; pollution prevention; energy efficiency; and inter-company partnering."[1]

Presidio National Park's sustainable community has a major focus on waste reduction, which includes pollution prevention as well as reuse and recycling. Portland, Oregon, has also emphasized waste

---

[1]The President's Council on Sustainable Development, *Eco-Efficiency Task Force Report*, 1996, Appendix B4, p. 4. Also, see Appendix B4 for good detailed descriptions of each of the aforementioned eco-industrial parks.

minimization and pollution prevention in its sustainability activities. For example, a recent Portland report on sustainable economic development suggests the idea of implementing "loan criteria which rewards businesses that . . . install source reduction or pollution prevention measures" to encourage more sustainable business practices.[2]

Whether or not a community explicitly uses the term pollution prevention, P2 is a critical building block for sustainability projects. The PCSD Task Force on Sustainable Communities makes a policy recommendation emphasizing the importance of P2, especially P2 partnerships: "Increase public-private pollution prevention efforts at the community level."[3]

RELEVANCE OF SUSTAINABLE COMMUNITY EFFORTS FOR P2 ACTIVITIES

Many pollution prevention activities have been implemented for years without any relationship to the notion of a sustainable community. How are such sustainable community activities, thereby, relevant to state and local government P2 activities and other organizations P2 activities? For an experienced P2 practitioner, what is the importance of sustainable community activities to his or her activities?

Sustainable community groups often create a vision for the community, such as identifying what their ideal community would look like in 20, 30, 50, or 100 years. This exercise can also create a vision for P2. For example, including more efficient natural resource use and zero emission industries helps set an overarching vision for P2 activities. These P2 activities are incorporated into the broader community perspective for developing a long-term healthy community. Such a vision helps more members of the community recognize the need for P2 activities.

---

[2]Patricia Scruggs and Philip Thompson, *Promoting Sustainable Economic Development in Portland: A Report to the Portland Development Commission*, Portland Development Commission, Portland, Oregon, October 1996, p. vii.

[3]The President's Council on Sustainable Development, *Sustainable Communities Task Force Report*, October 1996, Final Draft, p. 40.

Sustainable community initiatives can also help focus P2 efforts on difficult environmental problems, which are interrelated with social and economic problems. For example, many cities are addressing the complex issues of urban sprawl and traffic congestion. Such problems have significant environmental effects, such as air pollution and loss of natural habitat, yet these problems are affected by many different factors, such as our need for affordable and convenient transportation, housing prices, land development policies, love of the automobile, and individual choices of behavior. Addressing these social and economic factors along with the environmental factors in a systems approach allows the interrelationships to be more fully understood and analyzed. Such an integrated, holistic approach also could be invaluable in helping to develop and analyze potential solutions. Having different types of community members involved in the process in a sustainability effort also helps to determine whether the solution is politically feasible; also, the process can be used to negotiate and develop feasible alternatives. Project implementation is therefore more likely to succeed. For example, P2 practitioners who have tried to prevent mobile-source air pollution know how hard it is to address such issues in isolation from these broader community issues.

Sustainable community efforts also help industry, government, community groups and the general public work together to solve their community environmental problems. An example of such cooperation is the collaborative effort in eco-industrial parks. Unique partnerships can be created with individuals and organizations that P2 practitioners might have had less access to in the past. Such cooperation among many diverse stakeholders enables P2 projects to be undertaken by more individuals and organizations. For instance, more of the general public learns the importance of P2 and is motivated to help prevent pollution in their community.

TAKING ADVANTAGE OF SUSTAINABLE COMMUNITY ACTIVITIES

How can government P2 practitioners take advantage of sustainable community efforts? Sustainable community activities offer a great opportunity to generate more public support for P2 activities because sustainability and sustainable values create a broader emotional appeal and understanding of the need for P2. For instance, providing a long-term sustainable vision of what the community could look like in 100 years and what the current trends imply can help the public and other key stakeholders see the critical need for P2 as a tool for sustainability.

Similarly, sustainability activities can help to educate and motivate less-accessible audiences to participate in P2 activities. For instance, homeowners learn to reduce their household use of certain chemical products because they understand the long-term cumulative effect on their community from such usage.

Often, P2 activities are viewed mainly as addressing environmental and economic concerns and are focused on specific practices, policies, and technological solutions in factories, businesses, or homes. Sustainability can help focus some of the P2 activities on difficult long-term, diffuse, and/or multidisciplinary environmental problems, such as urban sprawl. Such problems may be solved only by implementing a range of policy mechanisms and technological solutions across a range of governmental departments and functional areas. Sustainability activities also enable government P2 practitioners to more easily work with other departments in such activities. For instance, the local environmental agency works with the transportation, planning, and economic development departments to address urban sprawl.

A related benefit is that sustainability also allows for more integration of P2 with other key community environmental efforts, such as ecosystem management and other natural resource issues. In many state and local governments, recreation and the protection and use of natural resources are handled by a natural resource agency, whereas P2 activities are conducted by the regulatory or a technical assistance agency. The natural resource agency addresses the more traditional flora and fauna issues such as ecosystem management, and the latter agency focuses more on technical engineering solutions to reduce the use of chemicals and other materials. This division can create a disconnect in the two efforts. Sustainable community activities can help foster the integration of the more traditional flora and fauna issues with those of P2. This integration enables identification of the interdependencies and leveraging of the two types of activities. For instance, Florida's Department of Environmental Protection (DEP) is implementing an ecosystem management strategy based on sustainability that integrates P2 activities. In fact, their ecosystem management definition includes pollution prevention.

This integration opportunity also applies to community economic efforts. Sustainable community initiatives can facilitate the incorporation of P2 principles into the activities of local economic development projects as, for instance, in the Brownsville, Texas, Eco-Industrial Park project.

Because of the many diverse stakeholders who participate in sustainability activities, such projects can help develop new innovative partnerships focused on P2. Such partnerships might involve the federal government, other state and local governments, industry, universities, community groups, trade associations, and individuals. Many collaboration examples have already been provided in this report, with diverse organizations such as the American Institute of Architects, the Department of Energy, the National Park Service, Cornell University, and The Nature Conservancy working with different communities across the country. These many different collaborations can help leverage scarce resources for P2. Such partners help provide manpower, information, funds, infrastructure, and expertise to help with P2 efforts related to community sustainability.

How government P2 officials can take advantage of sustainability projects depends on the unique factors of the community and its sustainability initiatives. For example, in a community focused on an eco-industrial park, such as in Baltimore, Maryland, it might be harder to try to do P2 projects with local residents. However, this eco-industrial park offers numerous opportunities for working with industry in P2. Similarly, a project like EcoVillage at Ithaca offers opportunities to educate, demonstrate, and teach residents about individual practices to prevent pollution.

Supporters of P2 have many different opportunities to leverage off sustainable community activities. However, such opportunities vary, depending on the unique community circumstances. So where and how does a P2 practitioner or other individual begin to take advantage of such opportunities?

SUGGESTED STEPS FOR TAKING ACTION

How can government P2 practitioners leverage scarce resources or expand their program focus using sustainable community activities? There are many ways that P2 practitioners and other individuals can start taking advantage of such sustainable community activities. How does an individual start to take action? Here are five suggested steps:

1. **Become more informed about the numerous references available regarding sustainable community activities.** There is a wide range of information available from traditional academic and technical sources, such as journal articles and universities, to hands-on practitioners who are implementing sustainability. The references for such information include academic, trade association, community and environmental groups, government literature, and World Wide Web (WWW) sites. For instance, the nonprofit educational organization called EcoCity Cleveland publishes a monthly newsletter with ideas and tools for a sustainable bioregion.[4] Another example is the Sustainable Communities Network World Wide Web site, developed with support from the Urban and Economic Development Division of EPA. This site contains a range of information including information about the fundamentals of sustainability, case studies, and links to sustainable community information on the net.

   Experts and other contacts within government at all levels, industry, universities, and NGOs are key sources of information. Examples of these types of sources are in the bibliography at the end of this report.

   To become familiar with sustainability information, be sure to identify sustainable community efforts in your own community and state. These activities are ones probably most easily take advantage of. However, lessons can also be learned from activities across the country or even the world.

---

[4]This monthly newsletter is called the *EcoCity Cleveland Journal*. To obtain a sample copy or to subscribe, contact EcoCity Cleveland at 216-932-3007.

2. **Develop specific ideas about how sustainable community efforts can help address your P2 needs.** What P2 needs and wants do you have today and in the future? What results do you ultimately want to achieve? How can sustainable community efforts help you in such activities? For example, if you want to focus more on mobile-source air pollution and your community has concerns over urban sprawl problems, study Seattle's and other sustainable community efforts that deal with such issues. Then identify whether and how sustainability might help you in your P2 activities related to mobile-source air emissions. Make a list of the most promising ideas that you might want to focus on through sustainability efforts.

3. **Identify key individuals, organizations, and businesses that are active or interested in sustainability and that are relevant to your needs.** For example, if you are very interested in activities related to pollution prevention in buildings because of a large amount of residential construction in your community, then identify organizations such as AIA, DOE, PTI, IBACOS, and the City of Austin. All of these have participated in activities to design, develop, test, and/or implement more sustainable practices in residential buildings. If you are interested in rural economic development and ecosystem management issues, identify organizations such as The Nature Conservancy, USDA, EPA, Florida DEP, Curry County, Oregon, and Northampton County, Virginia.

   Identifying key individuals and organizations that might create roadblocks to your efforts and involving them as stakeholders in the process can also be an important part of your process.

4. **Contact the organizations you have identified to help you implement your ideas.** These organizations may provide you only with information, but they may be able to offer technical assistance, manpower, and/or funding to help in your efforts. Also, identify creative ways that public-private partnerships might be formed to help implement your ideas.

5. **Act to implement your projects.** Such an action may first involve organizing a sustainable community initiative in your area, writing a grant proposal (such as in the Northampton County example), or just educating your own agency about the importance of sustainability. If there is already a sustainable community initia-

tive in your community, become an active member in it and start trying to integrate your project ideas into the ongoing agenda and activities.

As part of your action, it is important to include an evaluation component in your effort and to include the flexibility to revise your plans based on the evaluation results.

There are many ways to take advantage of the sustainable community "movement." These examples just highlight some ways to begin. The bibliography presents a sample structure for organizing information for this discovery process.

Chapter Seven

CONCLUSION

Although not coherently organized and still in an early stage of development, a sustainable community "movement" does exist in the United States. It manifests itself in hundreds of communities across the country, which are developing and implementing projects to create more sustainable communities for future generations by addressing social, economic, and environmental issues. Such projects occur in all types of communities—in large, medium, and small cities; in towns; in counties; and in rural communities. They are addressing a wide range of issues, as varied as urban sprawl, new economic development, inner city and brownfield redevelopment, local small businesses, a strong local economy, watershed planning, environmental justice, ecosystem management, agriculture, biodiversity, community spirit, and green buildings. This trend is likely to continue as more communities learn about sustainability practices and begin to apply them in their own communities.

Sustainable community efforts have an integrated and synergistic relationship to pollution prevention activities. Many communities consider P2 a building block toward sustainability. P2 may be part of the sustainability effort's goals and is often a main emphasis in the implementation of specific sustainable community projects. Sustainable community efforts also can create an overarching vision for P2.

Because of this relationship, sustainable community activities provide a great opportunity for local government and other pollution prevention practitioners to strengthen their programs. By exploiting the close relationship between sustainability activities and pollution prevention, P2 practitioners can

- Leverage scarce resources;

- Integrate P2 principles and practices into other key environmental efforts;

- Expand and integrate P2 activities throughout the community, including other local agency activities;

- Focus P2 efforts on difficult long-term, diffuse, and/or multidisciplinary environmental problems that interrelate with social and economic problems;

- Create a community-wide vision for P2;

- Provide a broader perspective on the need for P2;

- Generate more community support and interest in P2 activities;

- Educate and motivate less-accessible audiences to participate in P2 activities;

- Develop new innovative partnerships; and

- Help industry, government, community groups and the general public work together to solve their community environmental problems.

A wealth of information and resources exist for a P2 practitioner and other individuals who want to implement more sustainable practices in their communities. Resources for sustainability projects include information, funding, political and community support, man-hours, materials, expertise, and labor. These resources are available from many different sources including federal, state, and local governments; industry; professional associations; universities; and NGOs.

Individuals have many ways to take advantage of such sustainable community sources and opportunities. By prioritizing their individual needs and objectives, and exploring the relationships between these items and sustainable community activities, P2 practitioners and other individuals can identify priority areas to target in sustainable community efforts. Then they can contact the appropriate organizations to help them implement specific ideas. Regardless of the choice of action, state and local P2 practitioners should fully explore the sustainable community "movement" to help promote pollution prevention as a tool for sustainability.

There is an overwhelming amount of information about sustainability available through many different sources. It helps to organize and structure this information to focus the search for acquiring and absorbing such information. One useful organization of sustainability information for pollution prevention purposes is:

- General references
  - Integration of issues
  - Business/economic issues
  - Social/cultural issues
  - Management practices/governance
- Technology
- Environmental issues
  - Built environment
  - Transportation
  - Energy
  - Water and wastes
  - Flora and fauna
- Specific community examples

The bibliography is organized in this fashion to help the reader focus on areas that are most important to his or her own needs.

The first main area is general references. General references help provide an overview of the philosophy, theory, management, definitions, and practices related to sustainability. It is useful to begin by learning about some of the broader perspectives on sustainability. Such general references include the PCSD and the Center for Sustainability's tutorials. Since this report focuses on P2 issues, integration, business and economic, social and cultural, and governance and management issues are in this section. Such topics could easily be separate sections for other focuses related to sustainability.

The technology section refers to general issues about the role of technologies in sustainable community efforts, such as are mentioned in the National Environmental Technology Strategy. This section also includes some basic references about industrial ecology, and state and local government pollution prevention activities.

The environmental issues sections focus on organizing sustainability efforts into more traditional sector and community element categories, which are more relevant for P2 implementation needs. These issues include the built environment, transportation, energy, flora and fauna, and water and wastes. The built environment includes issues related to building construction and design. Transportation includes references related to transportation management, urban sprawl, cleaner cars, public transportation, mobile-source air pollution, etc. The energy section references include energy conservation, renewable energy, global warming, etc. Water and wastes include issues related to water, solid and hazardous waste management, watershed management, etc. Flora and fauna includes references related to agriculture, natural resource management, ecosystem management, etc.

Many references and some topics do not easily fit into one of these categories, such as DOE's Center of Excellence for Sustainable Development. This Center of Excellence for Sustainable Development obviously emphasizes energy issues; however, it is also a good source for general sustainability information. Its World Wide Web page for general sustainability information is a good starting place. However, the references have been organized in this fashion as a starting point for presenting the information. Such an organization helps if an individual is focused on a particular aspect of sustainability, such as agriculture and biodiversity or transportation and land use issues.

Last, some individual community references are presented to illustrate specific community progress, projects, and focus. Sources for the four detailed community examples cited in this report, i.e., Northampton County, Virginia; Seattle, Washington; EcoVillage at Ithaca, New York; and the Presidio, San Francisco, California; are presented in this section. A few other community and state references are also presented. Many of these states and communities have other documents and resources related to their efforts. This section presents a diverse sample of interesting sources. Also, some of the other references, such as the President's Council on Sustainable Development *Eco-Efficiency Task Force Report*, give other specific community examples.

This sample organization is a general one which the author felt was important for organizing information for P2 purposes. Each reader could develop his or her own structure. Developing one's own unique organizational structure can be helpful for focusing literature searches and individual priorities, since there is a wealth of information on sustainability in any one of these areas.

These sample references were chosen to show the range of information available to communities. It is also intended to be a good starting point to find out more information from the wide range of practitioners and other groups involved in a wide range of relevant activities.

GENERAL REFERENCES

This section includes interesting references on general sustainable community efforts. Also, it includes references related to business/economic issues, social and cultural issues, management practices and governance, and integration across different areas.

Center for Sustainability at the University of Washington WWW page for basic sustainable community information including a tutorial and references: http://weber.u.washington.edu/d43/common/.

Community Sustainability Resource Institute at 704-681-1955. An NGO working with communities in the Southeastern United States.

CONCERN, Inc., has sustainable community resource lists and materials; contact at 202-328-8160.

EPA Community-Based Environmental Protection WWW page: http://www.epa.gov/ecosystems/index.html.

EPA Office of Sustainable Ecosystems and Communities (OSEC). POC: Wendy Cleland-Hamnett, Director, Office of Sustainable Ecosystems and Communities, U.S. EPA, 202-260-4002, and Angela Nugent, Staff Director, Office of Sustainable Ecosystems and Communities, U.S. EPA, 202-260-5871. The OSEC WWW page is: http://www.epa.gov/ecocommunity/.

Environmental Sustainability Kit, prepared by the Pollution Prevention Alliance, the Environmental Defense Fund (EDF), Washington, D.C., October 1996. For more information, contact Meena Palaniappan at EDF at 202-387-3500.

The Global Cities Project at 415-775-0791, for case studies and handbooks for local government.

Goldman, Benjamin A., *Sustainable America: New Public Policy for the 21st Century,* Jobs and Environment Campaign, Cambridge, Massachusetts, 1995. Available through the National Technical Information Service, U.S. DOC, Springfield, Virginia, 703-487-4650.

Hren, Benedict J., and Diane M. Hren, *Community Sustainability: A Mini-Curriculum for Grades 9–12,* The Izaak Walton League of America, 1996; contact at 301-548-0150.

Indicators for sustainability WWW page by Maureen Hart: http://www.subjectmatters.com/indicators/index.html.

International Council for Local Environmental Initiatives, Gaithersburg, Maryland, an international environmental agency for local governments, WWW page: http://www.iclei.org/iclei.html.

Joint Center for Sustainable Communities, National Association of Counties and the United States Conference of Mayors: Jerry McNeil, Director, Community Services Division, NACo, 202-942-4237, and Dave Gatton, Senior Environmental Advisor, USCM, 202-293-7330.

Kemmis, Daniel, *Community and the Politics of Place*, University of Oklahoma Press, Norman and London, 1990.

Local government home page with direct links into organizations such as the National League of Cities and the National Association of Counties: http://www.localgov.org/.

Our Common Future, World Commission on Environment and Development (the Bruntland Commission), Oxford University Press, Oxford, 1987.

Public Technology, Inc., *Cities and Counties: Thinking Globally, Acting Locally, Sustainability in Action*, Washington, D.C., 1996.

The President's Council on Sustainable Development, 202-408-5296, or call 800-DOE-EREC to order PCSD reports. Their WWW page with access to information about its reports and activities is: http://www.whitehouse.gov/PCSD.

The President's Council on Sustainable Development, *Sustainable America: A New Consensus for Prosperity, Opportunity, and a Healthy Environment for the Future*, February 1996. Available from the PCSD at 202-408-5296 or call 800-DOE-EREC. This report is on the WWW at: http://www.whitehouse.gov/WH/EOP/pcsd/#council_report.

The President's Council on Sustainable Development, *Eco-Efficiency Task Force Report*, 1996. Available from the PCSD at 202-408-5296 or call 800-DOE-EREC or see its web site: http://www.whitehouse.gov/PCSD.

The President's Council on Sustainable Development, *Education for Sustainability: An Agenda for Action*, Washington, D.C., 1996. To obtain a copy of this report call the National Center for Environmental Publications and Information at 800-490-9198 and request publication # 238-R-96-002.

The President's Council on Sustainable Development, *Sustainable Communities Task Force Report*, Final Draft, Washington, D.C., October 1996. Available from the PCSD at 202-408-5296 or call 800-DOE-EREC.

Sargent, Frederic O., Paul Lusk, Jose A. Rivera, and Maria Varela, *Rural Environmental Planning for Sustainable Communities*, Island Press, Washington, D.C., 1991.

Sustainable Communities Network WWW page developed by the Sustainable Communities Network Partnership: http://www.sustainable.org/index.html.

TECHNOLOGY REFERENCES

Includes references related to technologies for sustainability, environmental technologies, pollution prevention, engineering, industrial ecology, etc.

Allenby, Braden R., and Deanna J. Richards, *The Greening of Industrial Ecosystems*, National Academy of Engineering, National Academy Press, Washington, D.C., 1994.

Bridge to a Sustainable Future: National Environmental Technology Strategy, Government Printing Office, Washington, D.C., April 1995. To obtain a copy of this document call 800-ENV-6676 or access it on the WWW at: http://www.gnet.org/gnet/gov/usgov/whitehouse/bridge/bridge.htm.

Center for Sustainable Development, Georgia Institute of Technology. This organization has developed a curriculum on sustainable development for engineering undergraduates. For more information contact Jorge A. Vanegas at 404-894-9881.

Environmental Technologies WWW page: http://www.gnet.org/GNET/.

Interagency Environmental Technology Office, a one-stop shop for federal agency environmental technology information. POC: Tom Houlihan at 202-408-5399, e-mail tom_houlihan@gnet.org, and FAX 202-408-6839.

Lachman, Beth, Robert Lempert, Susan Resetar, and Thomas Anderson, *Technology for a Sustainable Future, Ideas: A Summary of Workshop Discussions*, RAND, RP-417, 1995.

The National Pollution Prevention Roundtable, *The National Pollution Prevention Roundtable P2 Yellow Pages (The Green Yellow Pages)*, Washington, D.C., November 1995. Reference for state P2 organizations. For more information contact the NPPR at 202-466-P2P2.

The National Pollution Prevention Roundtable, *Preventing Pollution in our Cities and Counties: A Compendium of Case Studies*, Fall 1995. Examples of local government P2 activities. For more information contact the NPPR at 202-466-P2P2.

Public Technology, Inc., is a nonprofit technology organization for local governments. Its WWW page is: http://pti.nw.dc.us/.

Technology for a Sustainable Future: A Framework for Action, Government Printing Office, Washington, D.C., July 1994.

BUILT ENVIRONMENT REFERENCES

Includes references related to residential and commercial construction, building materials, urban design and development, etc.

American Institute of Architects (AIA) Environmental Design Charrette's WWW home page: http://www.aia.org/edc/homepage.htm.

American Solar Energy Society, *Buildings for a Sustainable America Case Studies*, Boulder, Colorado, n.d. Contact at 303-443-3130.

Beyond Shelter: Building Communities of Opportunity, the United States Report for Habitat II, U.S. Department of Housing and Urban Development, Rockville, Maryland, May 1996.

Civil Engineering Research Foundation, *Creating the 21st Century Through Innovation: Engineering and Construction for Sustainable Development, Executive Report*, Report #96-5016.E, Washington, D.C., 1996. Contact at 202-842-0555.

Global Environmental Options WWW page for sustainable buildings and communities information: http://www.geonetwork.org/.

Sustainable Building Sourcebook, Green Builder Program, Environmental and Conservation Services Department, Austin, Texas. Available on the WWW at: http://www.greenbuilder.com/sourcebook/SourcebookContents.html.

U.S. Green Building Conference—1994, National Institute of Standards and Technology, NIST Special Publication 863, U.S. Government Printing Office, Washington, D.C., June 1994. For more information on NIST publications, call 301-975-3058.

TRANSPORTATION-RELATED REFERENCES

Includes references related to transportation management, urban sprawl, land use, infrastructure development and management, cleaner cars, public transportation, mobile-source air quality issues, etc.

Beimborn, Edward, and Rob Kennedy, *Inside the Blackbox: Making Transportation Models Work for Livable Communities*, Citizens for a Better Environment, Milwaukee, Wisconsin, and the Environmental Defense Fund, Washington, D.C., August 1996.

Bernick, Michael, and Jason Munkres, *Designing Transit-Based Communities*, Institute of Urban and Regional Development, University of California at Berkeley, 1992.

Building Sustainable Communities, An Environment Guide for Local Government, Land Use: Stewardship and the Planning Process, The Global Cities Project, San Francisco, California, 1993. Contact at 415-775-0791.

Dutch government's transportation plan: *Second Transport Structure Plan: Transport in a Sustainable Society*, Part D: Government Decision, Second Chamber of the States-General, Session (the Netherlands), 1989–1990.

A Network of Livable Communities: Evaluating Travel Behavior Effects of Alternative Transportation and Community Designs for the

National Capital Region, Chesapeake Bay Foundation, Annapolis, Maryland, May 1996.

TransAct WWW site, Surface Transportation Policy Project site, contains information about transportation issues related to sustainability: http://www.transact.org/home.htm.

Weissman, Steve, and Judy Corbett, *Land Use Strategies for More Livable Places*, Local Government Commission, Sacramento, California, 1992.

ENERGY-RELATED REFERENCES

Includes references related to renewal energy, energy conservation, cleaner automobile fuels, global warming, etc.

Center of Excellence for Sustainable Development, DOE, WWW page for basic information including case study links: http://www.sustainable.doe.gov/.

CREST, the Center for Renewable Energy and Sustainable Technology's Solstice Internet Information Service: http://www.crest.org/.

Department of Energy. POC: William Becker, Center for Excellence for Sustainable Development, DOE, 303-275-4801, and Richard Burrow, DOE Headquarters Programmatic Activities, 202-586-1709.

Energy Efficiency and Renewable Energy Network, DOE, WWW page: http://www.eren.doe.gov/.

Hubbard, Alice, and Clay Fong, *Community Energy Workbook: Guide to Building a Sustainable Economy*, Rocky Mountain Institute, Snowmass, Colorado, 1995.

Rocky Mountain Institute, a nonprofit research and educational foundation that addresses efficient energy use with safe, sustainable sources as well as other resource issues. Its WWW site is: http://www.rmi.org/.

Sustainable Energy: A Local Government Planning Guide for a Sustainable Future, Urban Consortium Energy Task Force, Energy, Environment and Economic Development Unit, December 1992.

For a copy, call the Energy Efficiency and Renewable Energy Clearing House, 800-523-2929.

WATER- AND WASTES-RELATED REFERENCES

Includes references related to watershed management, water conservation, safe drinking water, coastal issues, waste reduction of solid waste and hazardous waste, recycling, etc.

Brownfields home page by EPA's Office of Solid Waste and Emergency Response, includes funding information about the National Brownfields Economic Redevelopment Pilots: http://www.epa.gov/brownfields/.

Chesapeake Bay Communities: Making the Connection, EPA for the Chesapeake Bay Program, Annapolis, Maryland, April 1996. A catalog of local initiatives to protect and restore the Chesapeake Bay watershed. Available through the WWW at the Chesapeake Bay Program local government site: http://www.epa.gov/r3chespk/cbp_home/localgov/localgov.htm.

EPA's Office of Wetlands, Oceans, and Watersheds WWW page: http://www.epa.gov/OWOW/index.html. An interesting document through this site is the Great Water Bodies Strategy document: http://www.epa.gov/OWOW/BODIES/content.html.

NOAA's Office of Sustainable Development and Intergovernmental Affairs. POC: John Bullard, Director, 202-482-3384. Also, NOAA's Coastal Zone Management Program. POC: Jeff Benoit, Director of the Office of Ocean and Coastal Resources Management, 301-713-3109.

Non-Hazardous Waste WWW page by EPA with information about municipal solid waste, household waste, recycling, and other waste issues: http://www.epa.gov/epaoswer/non-hw/index.htm.

Superfund Today, EPA's WWW page of Superfund information for communities: http://www.epa.gov/superfund/oerr/today/text%26gif/sftintro.htm.

Toward a Watershed Approach: A Framework for Aquatic Ecosystem Restoration, Protection, and Management, Coastal America, 1994. Contact Coastal America at 301-713-3160.

Watershed Management Program at EPA WWW site containing information about collaborative local, state, and regional watershed management approaches: http://www.epa.gov/OWOW/watershed/.

FLORA- AND FAUNA-RELATED REFERENCES

Includes references related to natural habitat, agriculture, ecosystem management, green spaces, conservation, using natural resources, park management, etc.

Alternative Agriculture, National Research Council, 1989.

The Alternative Farming Systems Information Center WWW page for sustainable agriculture information: http://www.inform.umd.edu:8080/EdRes/Topic/AgrEnv/AltFarm/.

The Ecosystem Approach: Healthy Ecosystems and Sustainable Economies, Volume I, Overview, Report of the Interagency Ecosystem Management Task Force, June 1995. Available through the National Technical Information Service, U.S. DOC, Springfield, Virginia, at 703-487-4650.

Grumbine, R. Edward, "What Is Ecosystem Management?" *Conservation Biology,* Volume 8, No. 1, March 1994.

Scott, Norman R., "Sustainable Development—An Evolutionary Concept," *Agriculture, Energy, Demand-Side Management, and Environmental Issues,* Proceedings from the 5th Cornell Agricultural Energy Program (CAEP) Conference, Albany, New York, May 1994.

Stevens, William K., *Miracle Under the Oaks: The Revival of Nature in America,* Pocket Books, New York, 1995. Interesting book about local habitat restoration activities.

United States Department of Agriculture. POC: Adella Backiel, Director of Sustainable Development, USDA, 202-720-2456, and Ruth McWilliams, Assistant Director for Cooperative Forestry,

USDA Forest Service, and Co-Chair for the USDA Working Group on Sustainable Rural Communities, 202-205-1373.

"Virginia Chapter News," *The Nature Conservancy,* Spring 1996.

Yaffee, Steven L., et al., *Ecosystem Management in the United States: An Assessment of Current Experience,* Island Press, Washington, D.C., 1996. Study includes points of contacts and brief descriptions of 105 ecosystem management projects throughout the United States.

SPECIFIC COMMUNITY REFERENCES

Burlington, Vermont, Office of the Mayor, Peter Clavelle, 802-865-7272.

Cambridge Civic Forums WWW page: http://civic.net/cambridge_civic_network/ccf/ccf.html.

Chattanooga's sustainability WWW page: http://www.chattanooga.net/SUSTAIN/index.html.

Curry County, Oregon, Sustainable Nature-Based Tourism Project. POC: Diane Kelsay, Egret Communications, Curry County Field Office, 541-332-3202.

EcoCity Cleveland, nonprofit organization that publishes monthly journal called, *EcoCity Cleveland Journal,* contact at 216-932-3007.

Eco-Industrial Park WWW page by Cornell University: http://www.cfe.cornell.edu/wei/EID.html. Contains basic background information and detailed information on the Fairfield (Baltimore, Maryland) and Trenton, New Jersey, EIPs.

EcoVillage at Ithaca References

EcoVillage at Ithaca, New York, *A Model for Land Conservation and Sustainable Neighborhood Development* WWW page: http://www.cfe.cornell.edu/ecovillage/.

Thomas, Gregory, *EcoVillage at Ithaca: Residents and Designers Working Together to Integrate Environmental Concerns into Housing Systems Design,* Presentation at Air & Waste Management Association 89th Annual Meeting & Exhibition, Nashville, Tennessee, June 1996. Contact A&WMA in Pittsburgh, Pennsylvania, at 412-232-3444.

Fairfield Ecological Industrial Park Strategic Plan: Work and Environment Initiative, Baltimore Development Corporation and Cornell University, August 1995. Fairfield Ecological Industrial Park is in Baltimore, Maryland.

The Green Institute, Minneapolis, Minnesota, 612-874-1148.

Lau, Sabrina M., *Investigating Eco-Industrial Park Development: Final Report and Recommendations for Future Consideration*, for the Green Institute, Minneapolis, Minnesota, October 1996. Survey of specific eco-industrial park activities.

Minnesota Sustainable Community References

> *Challenge for a Sustainable Minnesota: A Minnesota Strategic Plan for Sustainable Development*, Minnesota Sustainable Development Initiative, Minnesota Environmental Quality Board, St. Paul, Minnesota, Public Review Draft, July 1995. To access through the WWW: http://www.mnplan.state.mn.us/press/sustplan.html.

> *Common Ground: Achieving Sustainable Communities in Minnesota*, A Report to the Sustainable Economic Development and Environmental Protection Task Force to the Governor, the Minnesota Legislature, and the Minnesota Environmental Quality Board, St. Paul, Minnesota, September 1995.

> Minnesota Office of Environmental Assistance Sustainable Communities Team. POC: Diane Wanner, 612-215-0192.

Norberg-Hodge, Helena, *Ancient Futures: Learning from Ladakh*, Sierra Club Books, San Francisco, California, 1991. Interesting book about a traditional Eastern community which has relevance to U.S. sustainability efforts.

Northampton County, Virginia. POC: Timothy E. Hayes, Director of Sustainable Development, 757-678-0477. Also see Chesapeake

Bay Program/EPA Case Study locations such as: http://www.epa.gov/ecosystems/cases/osec.html#NORTH.

Portland, Oregon, Sustainable Community References

Portland Development Commission. POC: Susan Anderson, 503-823-7223.

Scruggs, Patricia, and Philip Thompson, *Promoting Sustainable Economic Development in Portland: A Report to the Portland Development Commission*, Portland Development Commission, Portland, Oregon, October 1996.

Presidio National Park, San Francisco, California, sustainability project. POC: Mike Savidge, 415-561-4491.

Steele County, Minnesota's, "Green Source 2020" Sustainable Community project. For more information contact Christine Renne, Steele County Environmental Services, 507-444-7475.

Seattle Sustainable Community References

Sustainability in Seattle 1995, A Report to the President's Council on Sustainable Development, a joint project by the Center for Sustainable Communities, Sustainable Seattle, and AtKisson & Associates, Inc., Seattle, Washington, 1995.

Sustainable Seattle at the Metrocenter YMCA. POC: Kara Palmer, 206-382-5013, at ext. 5072, and Lee Hatcher at ext. 5090; see also the group's WWW home page: http://www.scn.org/sustainable/susthome.html.

Virginia Sustainable Community References

Building on the Blueprint: How Virginia's Communities Are Implementing Sustainable Development, Environmental Law Institute, Washington, D.C., 1995.

Virginia Coastal Program supports several sustainable community projects. POC: Laura McKay, Program Manager, 804-698-4323.